Grammar and Punctuation

Grammar 2 Teacher's Guide

Carol Matchett

M000305218

Schofield & Sims

Free downloads available from the Schofield & Sims website

A selection of free downloads is available from the Schofield & Sims website (www.schofieldandsims.co.uk/free-downloads). These may be used to further enhance the effectiveness of the programme. The downloads add to the range of print materials supplied in the teacher's guides. They include the following items:

- a **Curriculum coverage chart**
- an enlarged **Focus text** for each lesson
- a **Dictation assessment sheet**
- a **Pupil target reminder**
- a **Learning pathways class chart** for each year group
- a **Final test analysis class chart** for each year group.

Published by **Schofield & Sims Ltd**, Dogley Mill, Fenay Bridge, Huddersfield HD8 0NQ, UK
Telephone 01484 607080
www.schofieldandsims.co.uk

This edition copyright © Schofield & Sims Ltd, 2017
First published in 2017

Author: **Carol Matchett**
Carol Matchett has asserted her moral rights under the Copyright, Designs and Patents Act, 1988, to be identified as the author of this work.

British Library Cataloguing in Publication Data
A catalogue record for this book is available from the British Library.

All rights reserved. Except where otherwise indicated, no part of this publication may be reproduced, stored in a retrieval system, or transmitted in any form or by any means, electronic, mechanical, photocopying, recording or otherwise, without either the prior permission of the publisher or a licence permitting restricted copying in the United Kingdom issued by the Copyright Licensing Agency Limited, Saffron House, 6–10 Kirby Street, London EC1N 8TS.

The **assessment resources** are exempt from these restrictions and may be photocopied after purchase, where indicated, for use within the purchaser's institution only.

Design by **Oxford Designers & Illustrators Ltd**

Printed in the UK by **Page Bros (Norwich) Ltd**

ISBN 978 0 7217 1393 9

Contents

Introduction

Schofield & Sims Grammar and Punctuation is a structured whole-school scheme for teaching grammar and punctuation while also building on vocabulary, reading and writing skills. It can be used alongside the **Schofield & Sims Spelling** series for complete Spelling, Punctuation and Grammar [SPaG] coverage.

Grammar and Punctuation is designed to progressively develop knowledge and understanding of grammatical concepts through six teacher's guides and six pupil books containing a carefully structured sequence of lessons. The teacher's guides provide you, the teacher or adult helper, with notes and activities to support the teaching of these lessons, annotated answers to the pupil book questions, and a variety of assessment resources for tracking progress.

Supporting a mastery approach, the focus of this programme is on rich practice, deep and secure understanding and fluency in application. Pupils not only learn the terminology and correct usage of grammar and punctuation, they also build up the skills, knowledge and confidence to apply them in their own independent writing. All pupils are encouraged to move at the same pace through the lessons and are given the same opportunity to fully understand the concept being taught. A wealth of practice questions, writing tasks, activity ideas and resources are provided to support the wider application of the grammar and punctuation that has been learnt in each lesson and to help pupils to truly master the art of writing.

The programme is designed primarily for pupils in Years 1 to 6, and the concepts and terminology that are introduced are in line with the National Curriculum for English. However, understanding of grammar and punctuation is cumulative, so grammatical terms and concepts introduced in one book are revisited and developed further in subsequent books to reinforce the pupils' understanding. In particular, concepts and areas of learning introduced towards the end of one book are revisited and embedded in the next book to further ensure consolidation and continuity.

There are 30 corresponding lessons in **Grammar 2** and its related **Teacher's Guide**, ten for each term. These lessons follow the statutory requirements for Year 2 'Vocabulary, grammar and punctuation' in the National Curriculum for English including Appendix 2, while also promoting and supporting other aspects of the English curriculum. A curriculum coverage chart is available to download from the Schofield & Sims website. An extended glossary can also be found at the back of this teacher's guide [pages 91–92], with a full list of all the terminology relevant to the Year 2 curriculum, along with clear explanations, examples and lesson references.

IMPLEMENTING THE TEACHING MODEL

The **Grammar 2 Teacher's Guide** supports explicit teaching of grammar and punctuation within the wider teaching of reading, writing and speaking. It is based on focused teaching sessions, using the following pedagogical model:

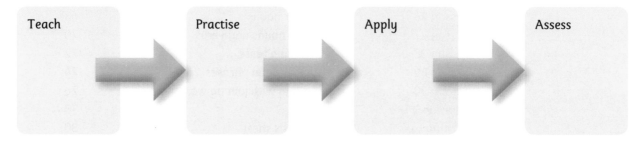

Teach → Practise → Apply → Assess

This teacher's guide supports an approach to teaching grammar and punctuation that is systematic, thorough and direct. It provides you with detailed **Teaching notes** for each lesson. A sample page is included below to show the structure of a typical lesson.

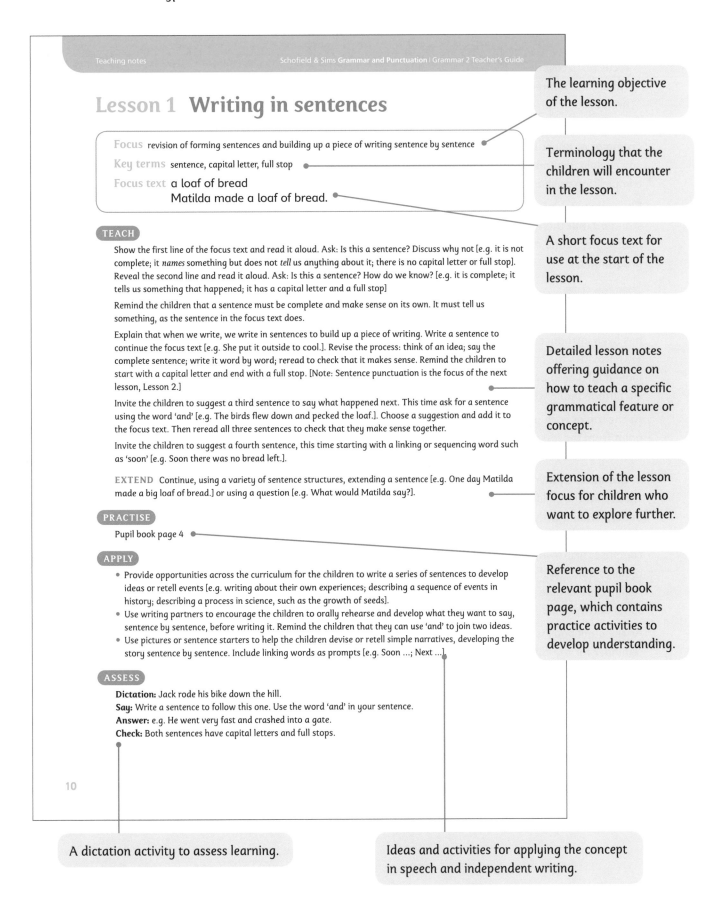

Teaching notes   Schofield & Sims **Grammar and Punctuation** | Grammar 2 Teacher's Guide

Lesson 1 Writing in sentences

Focus revision of forming sentences and building up a piece of writing sentence by sentence

Key terms sentence, capital letter, full stop

Focus text a loaf of bread
Matilda made a loaf of bread.

The learning objective of the lesson.

Terminology that the children will encounter in the lesson.

A short focus text for use at the start of the lesson.

TEACH

Show the first line of the focus text and read it aloud. Ask: Is this a sentence? Discuss why not [e.g. it is not complete; it *names* something but does not *tell* us anything about it; there is no capital letter or full stop]. Reveal the second line and read it aloud. Ask: Is this a sentence? How do we know? [e.g. it is complete; it tells us something that happened; it has a capital letter and a full stop]

Remind the children that a sentence must be complete and make sense on its own. It must tell us something, as the sentence in the focus text does.

Explain that when we write, we write in sentences to build up a piece of writing. Write a sentence to continue the focus text [e.g. She put it outside to cool.]. Revise the process: think of an idea; say the complete sentence; write it word by word; reread to check that it makes sense. Remind the children to start with a capital letter and end with a full stop. [Note: Sentence punctuation is the focus of the next lesson, Lesson 2.]

Invite the children to suggest a third sentence to say what happened next. This time ask for a sentence using the word 'and' [e.g. The birds flew down and pecked the loaf.]. Choose a suggestion and add it to the focus text. Then reread all three sentences to check that they make sense together.

Invite the children to suggest a fourth sentence, this time starting with a linking or sequencing word such as 'soon' [e.g. Soon there was no bread left.].

EXTEND Continue, using a variety of sentence structures, extending a sentence [e.g. One day Matilda made a big loaf of bread.] or using a question [e.g. What would Matilda say?].

Detailed lesson notes offering guidance on how to teach a specific grammatical feature or concept.

Extension of the lesson focus for children who want to explore further.

PRACTISE

Pupil book page 4

APPLY

- Provide opportunities across the curriculum for the children to write a series of sentences to develop ideas or retell events [e.g. writing about their own experiences; describing a sequence of events in history; describing a process in science, such as the growth of seeds].
- Use writing partners to encourage the children to orally rehearse and develop what they want to say, sentence by sentence, before writing it. Remind the children that they can use 'and' to join two ideas.
- Use pictures or sentence starters to help the children devise or retell simple narratives, developing the story sentence by sentence. Include linking words as prompts [e.g. Soon ...; Next ...].

Reference to the relevant pupil book page, which contains practice activities to develop understanding.

ASSESS

Dictation: Jack rode his bike down the hill.
Say: Write a sentence to follow this one. Use the word 'and' in your sentence.
Answer: e.g. He went very fast and crashed into a gate.
Check: Both sentences have capital letters and full stops.

10

A dictation activity to assess learning.

Ideas and activities for applying the concept in speech and independent writing.

TEACH

Each lesson begins with an introductory panel featuring the following information:

- **Focus** – The focus of the lesson is clearly stated.
- **Key terms** – The key terminology to be used in the teaching session is listed. Any new terminology that the children will come across for the first time in that lesson is highlighted in bold.
- **Focus text** – A short focus text is provided that has been designed for use at the start of the lesson. It is intended that the focus text is written or projected on to a whiteboard to be shared with the children. The focus texts cover a range of genres of writing and help to provide a context for the learning that allows the children to appreciate the purpose or effect of the target grammar or punctuation feature. All the focus texts are available for download from the Schofield & Sims website.

Clear guidance is given on how to use the **Focus text** at the start of the lesson to 'focus in' on the particular grammar or punctuation feature that you are teaching. The **Teaching notes** suggest possible ways that you can explain, demonstrate and discuss the feature to develop understanding. Sessions often involve some oral composition or shared writing, with the children involved in suggesting ideas and correcting mistakes.

The main teaching session covers the objectives that are required for the children to work at the expected standard, but there is also a suggestion for how you can **Extend** the focus for children who have grasped the main concept and are ready to delve deeper. These suggestions often provide a bridge to later lessons in the programme.

PRACTISE

Following the teaching session, the children are ready to practise the grammar or punctuation feature that has been introduced and clear page references are provided for the corresponding lesson in the pupil book. This provides the children with rich practice activities to consolidate their learning. The children can work individually or in pairs. In paired work, discussion between partners can help to develop understanding, encourage thoughtful answers and promote oral rehearsal.

At the top of each pupil book page a **Remember** panel provides a child-friendly summary of a key learning point from the lesson with examples that refer back to the **Focus text**. This acts as a reminder for the pupil and is also a useful reference for parents if sections of the pupil book are set as homework.

In **Grammar 2**, there are three pupil book activities for each lesson. The first **Try it** activity is designed to check that the children understand the key learning point; the second is designed to develop and use this understanding within sentences. You could do some of the activities orally, with the class or in groups, before the children write their answers. Each lesson then ends with a **Sentence practice** activity where the children compose their own sentence or sentences using the concept that has been taught in the lesson. If a child requires additional challenge, the **Sentence practice** could be extended by increasing the number of sentences required. A sample page from the pupil book is included on page 7. It shows the structure of a typical page and some of the main features.

As the pupil book is completed, it will form an ongoing record of the child's progress. It will also be a useful reminder for the child when writing independently.

Answers to all the pupil book activities are provided in the teacher's guide. Alongside the answers you will also find detailed annotations offering guidance on what to look out for and how to tackle potential problems, as well as suggestions for discussing or comparing the children's answers.

There are **Revision** pages at the end of each section of the pupil book. In **Grammar 2**, these pages revise concepts introduced in **Grammar 1** as well as material from earlier sections of the current book, making sure that learning is not forgotten. The focus of each revision activity is given on the **Answers** pages in the teacher's guide to help you identify areas where the children might need further revision.

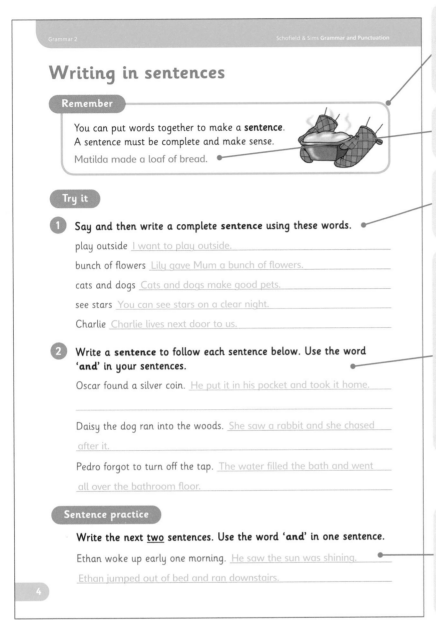

The **Remember** panels provide a child-friendly summary of the key learning point for the page.

Examples are given that refer back to the **Focus text**.

The first **Try it** activity checks for understanding of the key learning point.

The second **Try it** activity develops the children's understanding and allows them to practise using the new learning in context. You could do some of these activities orally before the children write their own answers [e.g. orally rehearsing sentences or discussing choice of words].

Each lesson ends with **Sentence practice**, where the children compose their own sentence or sentences using the key learning point.

APPLY

A challenge when teaching grammar and punctuation is ensuring that children transfer learning from grammar lessons into their own writing. This is why the **Teaching notes** always provide a list of suggestions for activities where the children might apply their new learning in written, or sometimes oral, composition. These opportunities may be in English lessons or across the curriculum. You can use these suggestions as and when appropriate and you should also look for opportunities to embed learning in the writing activities you already have planned.

It is important to establish the expectation that what has been taught and practised in a grammar and punctuation lesson is applied when writing. This can be helped by setting targets for writing that relate to a specific grammar and punctuation concept that has been taught, and referring to these before, during and after writing, especially in marking and feedback. You will find further support for target-setting on page 9.

At the end of each section of the pupil book there is a short **Writing task**. This again helps to make explicit the link between the grammar and punctuation lessons and the children's own writing. The task provides an opportunity for the children to apply, or 'show off', what they have learnt about grammar and punctuation by using it in written composition. It can be used as a starting point for further creative writing or topic-based activities. There is more information about how to use and assess the **Writing task** on page 8.

ASSESS

Regular assessment is crucial to check understanding, reflect on learning and monitor progress. It is important that teachers know what the children have learnt, what they are finding difficult and what they need to know next. This helps inform teaching, planning and target-setting. **Grammar 2** and its related **Teacher's Guide** offer frequent opportunities and a range of resources for in-school assessment, which can be used flexibly in line with your own school's assessment policy.

Ongoing assessment

At the end of each page of the **Teaching notes** you will find a short assessment task based around a dictation exercise. This is designed to be used once the children have completed the relevant lesson in the pupil book and begun to apply the new learning in their writing. The children are required to write and punctuate a dictated sentence or sentences. They are often then asked to change or annotate the sentence in some way, following verbal prompts. This dictation task is designed to show whether the children have understood the terminology and the key learning objective of the lesson. Sometimes previous learning is also checked. A **Dictation assessment sheet** is available to download from the Schofield & Sims website.

Periodic assessment

The **Writing task** at the end of each section in the pupil book allows for a more formal assessment of how the children are applying their cumulative knowledge of sentence structure, grammar and punctuation in their own writing.

At Key Stage 1, you should introduce and discuss the task with the children before they begin writing. You may feel that some tasks need more of an introduction than others [e.g. discussing ideas when the children are asked to write an imaginary sequence of events]. You should not, however, orally rehearse sentences that the children might write, as putting ideas into complete sentences is part of the assessment.

Included in the teacher's guide is an **Analysis sheet** for each **Writing task** [pages 32, 56 and 80]. This lists relevant criteria relating to punctuation, and to grammar and sentence structure based on what has been taught to date. Look for each criterion in the child's completed **Writing task** and record whether there is no evidence, some evidence or clear evidence of the use of that feature in the piece of writing. Photocopies of these sheets can also be used to analyse other samples of writing to give a better picture of a child's abilities.

Also included is a **Pupil checklist** for each **Writing task** [pages 33, 57 and 81]. This is designed to encourage the children's self-assessment and also allows you to give targeted feedback. As the children complete the checklist you could ask them to annotate their writing to show where they have successfully used a particular grammar or punctuation feature [e.g. circling the capital letters they have used].

Whether you choose to use the **Analysis sheet** or the **Pupil checklist**, both include a space for you to record a future target for the child. This is an important part of the writing assessments: identifying strengths and weaknesses and informing future teaching. Any problems or misunderstandings that are noted should be addressed and targets updated based on the evidence.

Summative assessment

There is a **Final test** provided as a photocopiable resource on pages 82–85 of this teacher's guide. This is designed to be used as an end-of-year assessment when all or most of the sections of the pupil book are complete. It is similar in style to the short answer test in the end of Key Stage 1 National Tests and it covers all the content introduced in the programme so far. You can use it to help check the children's learning and whether their progress is in line with expectations.

A **Mark scheme** for the **Final test** is provided on pages 86–87 and gives the answers and assessment focus of each question. The **Analysis sheet** for the **Final test** allows you to record the children's marks and will be helpful in identifying individual or class strengths and areas that might need to be revisited. This can be found on page 88 and a whole-class version is available to download from the Schofield & Sims website.

Tracking progress

A number of resources are provided at the back of the teacher's guide and as downloadable resources to further support assessment of learning, tracking progress and record-keeping.

Following a **Writing task**, if a group of children require further focused support on a particular writing target, the **Target tracking sheet** on page 89 can be used to note evidence of progress towards that target. You should look for evidence of progress in independent writing in English and in other subjects. Judgements should not be made solely on one piece of writing.

Pupil name	Evidence from independent writing	Progress in independent writing
Sarah Jacobs	Paragraph on 'My family'. Book review of 'The Nightingale'. Science report on 'Habitats'.	① ② ③

The target should be reviewed after a set period of time to see if it has been achieved. A new target might then be set, or further teaching and reinforcement opportunities planned as necessary. A **Pupil target reminder** is available to download from the Schofield & Sims website. This can be placed on a child's desk as a prompt to remind them of their current writing target.

The **Learning pathways sheet** on page 90 acts as an at-a-glance overview of where a child is in their learning. If completed at regular intervals [e.g. at the end of every term] it allows you to track the progress that has been made and to identify areas where further support might be needed. Alternatively it can be completed just once at the end of the year to act as a useful summative record for the child's subsequent teacher. The chart shows criteria in line with the expected standards for Year 2. Circles are ticked to show the depth of the child's understanding. These judgements should be made using a variety of evidence, including a number of examples of independent writing. Learning is only definitely embedded when the concept is always or nearly always present based on evidence from a range of writing tasks. A **Learning pathways class chart**, available to download from the Schofield & Sims website, allows you to keep a record of progress for the whole class in one spreadsheet.

The children should also be encouraged to reflect on their own learning at regular intervals, saying what they have learnt and how they have used it in their writing. There is a **Progress chart** at the back of the pupil book where pupils can record their progress through the programme by ticking the circle when they feel they have achieved the content of the statement.

Lesson 1 Writing in sentences

Focus revision of forming sentences and building up a piece of writing sentence by sentence

Key terms sentence, capital letter, full stop

Focus text **a loaf of bread**
Matilda made a loaf of bread.

TEACH

Show the first line of the focus text and read it aloud. Ask: Is this a sentence? Discuss why not [e.g. it is not complete; it *names* something but does not *tell* us anything about it; there is no capital letter or full stop]. Reveal the second line and read it aloud. Ask: Is this a sentence? How do we know? [e.g. it is complete; it tells us something that happened; it has a capital letter and a full stop]

Remind the children that a sentence must be complete and make sense on its own. It must tell us something, as the sentence in the focus text does.

Explain that when we write, we write in sentences to build up a piece of writing. Write a sentence to continue the focus text [e.g. She put it outside to cool.]. Revise the process: think of an idea; say the complete sentence; write it word by word; reread to check that it makes sense. Remind the children to start with a capital letter and end with a full stop. [Note: Sentence punctuation is the focus of the next lesson, Lesson 2.]

Invite the children to suggest a third sentence to say what happened next. This time ask for a sentence using the word 'and' [e.g. The birds flew down and pecked the loaf.]. Choose a suggestion and add it to the focus text. Then reread all three sentences to check that they make sense together.

Invite the children to suggest a fourth sentence, this time starting with a linking or sequencing word such as 'soon' [e.g. Soon there was no bread left.].

EXTEND Continue, using a variety of sentence structures, extending a sentence [e.g. One day Matilda made a big loaf of bread.] or using a question [e.g. What would Matilda say?].

PRACTISE

Pupil book page 4

APPLY

- Provide opportunities across the curriculum for the children to write a series of sentences to develop ideas or retell events [e.g. writing about their own experiences; describing a sequence of events in history; describing a process in science, such as the growth of seeds].
- Use writing partners to encourage the children to orally rehearse and develop what they want to say, sentence by sentence, before writing it. Remind the children that they can use 'and' to join two ideas.
- Use pictures or sentence starters to help the children devise or retell simple narratives, developing the story sentence by sentence. Include linking words as prompts [e.g. Soon ...; Next ...].

ASSESS

Dictation: Jack rode his bike down the hill.
Say: Write a sentence to follow this one. Use the word 'and' in your sentence.
Answer: e.g. He went very fast and crashed into a gate.
Check: Both sentences have capital letters and full stops.

Pupil book answers

Writing in sentences

Remember

You can put words together to make a **sentence**.
A sentence must be complete and make sense.

Matilda made a loaf of bread.

Try it

1 Say and then write a complete **sentence** using these words.

play outside I want to play outside.

bunch of flowers Lily gave Mum a bunch of flowers.

cats and dogs Cats and dogs make good pets.

see stars You can see stars on a clear night.

Charlie Charlie lives next door to us.

These are just examples of sentences that include the given words. There are many different possibilities so you could compare the children's answers.

To be correct, a sentence should make sense and have a capital letter and full stop. Any names used should also have capital letters.

2 Write a **sentence** to follow each sentence below. Use the word '**and**' in your sentences.

Oscar found a silver coin. He put it in his pocket and took it home.

Daisy the dog ran into the woods. She saw a rabbit and she chased after it.

Pedro forgot to turn off the tap. The water filled the bath and went all over the bathroom floor.

These are example answers. Accept any sentence that makes sense, follows on from the given sentence and includes the word 'and'.

Check that the sentence begins with a capital letter and ends with a full stop.

Sentence practice

Write the next <u>two</u> sentences. Use the word '**and**' in one sentence.

Ethan woke up early one morning. He saw the sun was shining. Ethan jumped out of bed and ran downstairs.

4

This is an example answer. Both sentences must make sense, and follow on from each other. They could begin with a linking word [e.g. Next ...]. One sentence must include the word 'and'. Both sentences must have a capital letter and full stop.

Lesson 2 Sentence punctuation

Focus checking that the start and end of sentences are correctly demarcated

Key terms sentence, punctuation, capital letter, full stop, question mark, exclamation mark

Focus text the little rabbit waited for his friend Ben he waited and he waited the little rabbit began to worry where could Ben be

TEACH

Show the focus text. Read it aloud as it is written, with no pauses or punctuation. Ask: Does it sound right? Why not? [e.g. there is no punctuation to show pauses; it is confusing because we do not know where one sentence ends and another starts; it sounds mixed up]

Read the text so that the four sentence breaks can be heard. Ask the children to put up their hands when they hear the end of a sentence. Use a coloured pen to add the capital letter and full stop at the start and end of each sentence. Discuss the last sentence. Ask: What is needed here? [a question mark]

Remind the children that we use capital letters and full stops to show where sentences start and end. Explain that sentence punctuation is important because it clearly separates the sentences in a piece of writing. This makes the writing easier to follow and understand – as shown by the focus text.

Sometimes we use a question mark or exclamation mark instead of a full stop. Ask the children to explain why [e.g. question marks for questions; exclamation marks to show strong feelings].

Remind the children to punctuate sentences as they write them. Explain that they should also read back over what they have written, listening for sentence breaks to check that the correct sentence punctuation is in place. Discuss common mistakes [e.g. adding the full stops but forgetting the capital letters; adding a full stop and then continuing with 'and']. Remind the children that 'and' joins ideas to make one longer sentence.

EXTEND Help the children to proofread their own writing, checking that they have used correct sentence punctuation.

PRACTISE

Pupil book page 5

APPLY

- Set proofreading targets that apply to all writing, across the curriculum [e.g. check that sentences begin with a capital letter; check that sentences end with a full stop, '?' or '!'].
- Encourage the children to rehearse sentences orally before writing them. Aim to make using a full stop and capital letter an automatic part of the 'Say it/Write it' process.
- Let the children read their work aloud to a partner so they can hear the sentence breaks and add any missing punctuation.
- Ask the children to write a given number of sentences [e.g. four or five] on a particular subject, so there is a clear focus on sentence boundaries.

ASSESS

Dictation: The twins are waiting by the door. Mum will be home soon and they will have tea.
Say: Read what you have written. Check the sentence punctuation.
Check: The sentence boundaries are correctly identified. Both sentences are correctly punctuated with capital letters and full stops.

Pupil book answers

Sentence punctuation

Remember

All sentences start with a **capital letter**. Most sentences end with a **full stop**. Some sentences end with a **question mark** or an **exclamation mark**.

The little rabbit began to worry. Where could Ben be?

Try it

1 Write in the missing **punctuation marks**.

We went to the zoo. Jacob was very excited.

The clown did a clever trick and Abdul laughed at him.

Gran came to visit us last Monday. Grandpa came too.

Who was knocking at the door? Max went to see.

He made a boat out of wood and sailed it on the sea.

Check that the children have identified the sentence boundaries correctly. If they are having difficulties, encourage them to read the sentences aloud.

Make sure there is no full stop added before 'and'.

2 Here is part of a story. The **sentence punctuation** is missing. Write the story using the correct punctuation.

The children went to find Nina they looked in the garden and they looked in the shed they looked everywhere where was Nina

The children went to find Nina. They looked in the garden and they looked in the shed. They looked everywhere. Where was Nina?

Check that the four sentences have been identified and correctly demarcated.

Make sure there is no full stop added before 'and'.

Sentence practice

Write <u>three</u> sentences about your favourite toy.

My favourite toy is my Aston Villa football. I got it for my birthday. I play with it in the playground with my friends.

5

This is an example of three sentences correctly demarcated with capital letters and full stops.

Check that the sentence boundaries are correctly identified, including for any sentences using 'and'. Capital letters should be used for 'I' and at the start of any names. [Note: This was covered in **Grammar 1**.]

Lesson 3   Joining words: 'and', 'but'

Focus composing sentences using the co-ordinating conjunctions 'and', 'but'

Key terms sentence, joining word

Focus text There were three bowls of porridge and they all smelt delicious. She tried the porridge in the first bowl but it was too hot.

TEACH

Show the focus text and read it aloud. Ask: Do you recognise the story? Which part of the story is it? Ask: How many sentences are there? [two] Circle the capital letter and full stop at the start and end of each sentence to show the two sentences clearly.

Discuss how the words 'and' in the first sentence and 'but' in the second sentence join together two separate ideas in one sentence. Read the text without these words so the children hear how it would sound as four separate sentences. Discuss why we use 'joining words' in this way [e.g. it sounds smoother; it is more like a written story; it links ideas together].

Explain that the joining words 'and' and 'but' are used to join together two separate sentences to make one longer sentence. [Note: 'And' and 'but' are co-ordinating conjunctions which join together two main clauses. However, at this stage the children do not need to know this terminology so they are called joining words in **Grammar 1** and **2**. You can use the term 'conjunction' if you wish.]

The children should already be familiar with using 'and' to add another word or idea on to a sentence. [Note: This is covered in **Grammar 1**.] Ask the children to orally compose a different ending for the first sentence of the focus text using 'and' [e.g. There were three bowls of porridge and Goldilocks was very hungry.].

Discuss how using 'but' is different [e.g. in the focus text 'but' introduces an unexpected problem]. Explain that 'but' is used when the second idea is a contrast [something different or a change], not a simple addition. Invite the children to orally compose a third sentence for the story using 'but' [e.g. She tasted the porridge in the second bowl but it was too sweet.]. Ask: What about the next sentence – would we use 'and' or 'but'? [e.g. She tasted the porridge in the third bowl and it was just right.]

EXTEND Compose a sentence using both 'and' and 'but'.

PRACTISE

Pupil book page 6

APPLY

- When reading stories, collect examples of sentences using 'but' [e.g. He may be small but he is mighty.]. Use these as models for the children to write their own sentences.
- The children write riddles using 'but' [e.g. It has legs but it cannot run.].
- The children write imaginative sentences using a sentence starter [e.g. I opened the box and …].
- In other subjects, ask the children to write comparisons using 'and' and 'but' [e.g. comparing living things in science – 'Brown bears and polar bears … Brown bears live in … but polar bears …'].

ASSESS

Dictation: Mum went to post a letter. She did not have a stamp.

Say: Write this as one sentence using a joining word.

Answer: Mum went to post a letter but she did not have a stamp.

Check: The correct joining word is chosen and the sentence is correctly punctuated.

Pupil book answers

Joining words: 'and', 'but'

Remember

The words '**and**' and '**but**' are **joining words**. They join together two sentences to make one longer sentence.

She saw the porridge and it smelt delicious.

She tasted the porridge but it was too hot.

Try it

1 Choose the best **joining word, 'and'** or **'but'**, to complete each sentence.

She opened the door _____and_____ they went inside.

I can swim a width _____but_____ I cannot dive in.

Ali found a wooden chest _____but_____ it was locked.

A car came down the road _____and_____ it stopped outside.

He waited _____and_____ he waited _____but_____ no-one came.

2 Add the **joining word 'but'** and then complete each **sentence**.

The rabbit was only small but he was brave.

I like grapes but I do not like bananas.

I wanted to go skating but the ice rink was closed.

Lucy was winning the race but she fell over.

A spider has eight legs but a ladybird has six legs.

Sentence practice

Write a sentence about a monster using the word '**but**'.

The monster was big but he did not scare us.

6

The children could use 'and' instead of 'but' in the third and fifth sentences. Encourage them to think about whether the second part of the sentence follows on from the first or contrasts with it.

These are example sentences. Check that 'but' introduces something that contrasts with the first part of the sentence. Compare the children's answers.

Check that sentences are correctly punctuated with a full stop at the end.

This is an example of a possible sentence. The sentence should make sense and be correctly punctuated.

Compare the children's different sentences and how they use the word 'but'.

Lesson 4 Joining words: 'or'

Focus using the co-ordinating conjunction 'or'

Key terms sentence, joining word

Focus text

> We can eat the porridge now or we can go for a walk.

> We should not be long or the porridge will get cold.

> Do you like porridge hot or cold?

TEACH

Show the focus text. Read aloud the sentences in the speech bubbles. Discuss which character might be speaking.

Point out the new joining word used in these sentences [or]. Read the first sentence as two separate sentences so the children can hear how 'or' joins the two ideas or sentences to make one longer sentence. Discuss why 'or' has been used in this sentence [e.g. it introduces a choice or an alternative].

Explain that 'or' is another joining word like 'and' and 'but'. It can join together two ideas or sentences to make one longer sentence, as in the first two sentences of the focus text. It can also be used to join two words, as in the third sentence of the focus text.

Explain that each joining word [and, but, or] has its own special function. We cannot use 'and' or 'but' in the focus text. Demonstrate this by reading the focus text with 'and' or 'but' in place of 'or' [e.g. We should not be long and the porridge will be cold.]. It does not make sense: 'and' is for adding another thing rather than introducing a choice between two things.

Use the sentences in the focus text to discuss when to use 'or'. This might be when talking about alternatives [e.g. We can … or we can …; hot or cold], or when expressing what might happen [e.g. We should not … or …].

Provide some other sentences using 'or' for the children to complete [e.g. We could have porridge or …; Don't eat boiling hot porridge or …; Is the porridge lumpy or …?].

EXTEND Challenge the children to write sentences containing all three of the joining words [e.g. I will have toast and jam but I don't want porridge or eggs.].

PRACTISE

Pupil book page 7

APPLY

- In factual writing, encourage the children to use 'or' to give alternatives [e.g. Woodlice live under logs or leaves.].
- Provide opportunities for writing about choices. You could ask: What shall we do to make the playground more attractive? [We could … or we could …]; or: What might this character do next in the story? [He might … or he might …].
- Set a target for writing across the curriculum [e.g. to use 'and', 'but' and 'or' to construct sentences].

ASSESS

Dictation: I want a pet dog. Mum says dogs are messy. I can have a fish. I can have a rabbit.

Say: Write the four sentences as two sentences. Use two different joining words.

Answer: e.g. I want a pet dog but Mum says dogs are messy. [She says] I can have a fish or I can have a rabbit.

Check: The two new sentences are punctuated correctly and use appropriate joining words.

Pupil book answers

Joining words: 'or'

Remember

The word '**or**' is another **joining word**. You can use 'or' to join two words or to join two sentences to make one longer sentence.

Do you like porridge hot or cold?

We can eat the porridge now or we can go for a walk.

Try it

1 Choose the best **joining word**, '**or**', '**and**' or '**but**', to complete each sentence.

We can stay here ____or____ we can go to the park.

You must go now ____or____ the giant will eat you.

I went to buy some jam ____but____ the shop was shut.

The mouse saw the cat ____and____ it ran and hid.

Take the cake out of the oven ____or____ it will burn.

2 Add the **joining word 'or'** and then complete each **sentence**.

We could hide in the shed or behind the bins.

Apples can be red or green.

It might rain or it might be sunny.

We can play inside or we can go outside.

The box is under the bed or it might be by the door.

These are example sentences. Check that 'or' introduces a choice, an alternative or an idea that makes sense. Discuss different ideas.

Check that sentences are correctly punctuated with a full stop at the end.

Sentence practice

Write a sentence about what you might do after school. Use the word '**or**'.

I might read my new book or I might play on the computer.

This is an example of a sentence using 'or'. The sentence should make sense and be correctly punctuated with a capital letter and full stop.

Lesson 5 Verbs: past and present tense 1

> Focus recognising verbs in sentences; introducing the terms 'past tense', 'present tense'
>
> Key terms verb, **tense, past tense, present tense**
>
> Focus text I open the door. I jump over the cat. I dash down the road. I climb over the fence. I turn the corner and I bump into the postman.

TEACH

Show the focus text and read it aloud. Invite the children to mime the actions. Ask: Which words tell us the actions in these sentences? [e.g. the highlighted words; the verbs; the 'doing words']

Read the focus text again. Ask: Are these actions happening right now or in the past? [right now]

Explain that verbs [doing words] are very important in sentences. Firstly, they tell us about actions, what is happening or what someone is doing. A sentence does not make sense without a verb – so, for example, the focus text would not make sense without the highlighted words. Secondly, the verb tells us *when* something happened.

Introduce the term 'tense': explain that it means *when* something happened. Explain that all verbs have a present tense and a past tense. The present tense form shows that the action is happening right now, or in the present; the past tense form shows that it happened before, or in the past.

The verbs in the focus text are in the present tense – as if the events are happening right now. Write the word 'Yesterday' at the start of the focus text and begin to change the verbs into the past tense [opened, jumped]. Ask the children what they notice [e.g. you are adding –ed to the verbs]. Establish that in the past tense many verbs have the ending –ed added to them. Invite the children to change the remaining verbs in the focus text. Ask them to suggest other verbs that follow this pattern.

EXTEND Look through stories for past tense verbs that do *not* end with –ed. [Note: This is covered in the next lesson, Lesson 6.] Make lists of past tense verbs ending with –ed and other past tense forms.

PRACTISE

Pupil book page 8

APPLY

- Refer to tense when the children are writing in other subjects [e.g. in history, use the past tense to write accounts of events or people's lives; in geography, use the present tense to write about other countries].
- Remind the children to use the past tense when planning, telling, orally rehearsing and writing stories.
- Together, write lists of past tense verbs that might be useful for a piece of writing.
- The children write a short personal account of an event, underlining all the past tense verbs ending with –ed.
- Look for times when the children use the wrong tense for a verb and prompt them to change it.

ASSESS

Dictation: Jake plays the trumpet and Eve bangs her drum.
Say: Underline the two verbs. These verbs are in the present tense. Write them in the past tense.
Answer: played, banged
Check: The two verbs are identified and the past tense verbs spelt correctly. The sentence is correctly punctuated, including capital letters for names.

Pupil book answers

Verbs: past and present tense 1

Remember

Verbs are doing words. Verbs can be in the **past tense** or the **present tense**. The **tense** of the verb shows when it happened.

I open the door.   (present tense – happening now)
I opened the door.   (past tense – happened in the past)

Try it

1 Underline the **verb** in each of these sentences. Write whether it is in the **past tense** or the **present tense**.

Thunder <u>boomed</u> across the roof tops. ___past___ tense

Caterpillars <u>turn</u> into butterflies. ___present___ tense

He <u>followed</u> the trail of stones. ___past___ tense

The girl <u>jumps</u> into the stream. ___present___ tense

2 The **verbs** in these sentences are in the **present tense**. Rewrite each sentence in the **past tense**.

I count six trees. I counted six trees.

He waits for the bus. He waited for the bus.

Ellie scores a goal. Ellie scored a goal.

Sam crosses the road. Sam crossed the road.

We share the sweets. We shared the sweets.

> The past tense verbs must be spelt correctly, including those with a final –e [i.e. scored, shared].
>
> Look out for any errors showing that the children do not understand that –ed is the ending added to verbs to show past tense [e.g. crosst; waitid]. It is important to secure this concept.

Sentence practice

Write <u>two</u> sentences using the **verb** 'walk'. Write one in the **present tense** and one in the **past tense**.

I walk to school every day.

The old man walked up the hill.

8

These are examples of acceptable sentences. The word 'walk' must be used as a verb and not as a noun [e.g. *not* 'I went for a walk.']. The past tense verb must be spelt correctly and sentences must be correctly punctuated.

Lesson 6 Verbs: past and present tense 2

Focus using past and present tense; introducing irregular past tense verbs

Key terms verb, tense, past tense, present tense

Focus text He runs down the road. He takes a left turn. He goes into the park. He is tired. He sees a bench. He has a rest. He falls asleep.

TEACH

Show the focus text. Discuss the actions of the character [e.g. What does he do first? Then what?]. Ask the children to look at the highlighted words. Ask: What can you tell me about these words? [e.g. they are all verbs; they are in the present tense]

At this point explain that words such as 'is' and 'has', which do not name an action, are still verbs. They are sometimes described as 'being words' rather than 'doing words'. Like all verbs, they are needed for the sentence to make sense and they also have a present and past tense.

Invite the children to help you change the verbs into the past tense so that the focus text sounds like a story. Discuss whether 'runned down the road' sounds right. What would we say? [ran]

Explain that all verbs have a past and present tense but not all past tense verbs end with –ed. Sometimes the past tense form changes in different ways [e.g. the middle vowel changes in 'run – ran']. Lots of verbs we use all the time are like this and it is important to know their past tense forms. Go through the remaining verbs in the focus text discussing the past tense form of each verb.

Children usually learn these irregular forms naturally through hearing and reading them. Try saying some more irregular verbs in a sentence and see if they can say or write the past tense version [e.g. I make a noise. I dig a hole. I eat my dinner. I swim. I fly.].

EXTEND Collect and learn the past tense of other irregular verbs [e.g. fight – fought; catch – caught].

PRACTISE

Pupil book page 9

APPLY

- Draw attention to irregular past tense verbs when reading stories or accounts. Make lists.
- Use writing partners to encourage the children to check for irregular verbs in their own stories or accounts, by reading aloud and listening for verbs that do not sound right [e.g. He growed and growed.].
- In history, the children write pairs of sentences comparing life in the past and life today [e.g. Today we write on … In Victorian times children wrote on …; Today we wear … Back then they wore …].
- The children write a sentence for each day of the week using an irregular verb [e.g. On Monday I went to …; On Tuesday it was …; On Wednesday Joe came …; On Thursday we made …].

ASSESS

Dictation: It is morning and the sun comes up over the trees.
Say: Underline the two present tense verbs in the sentence. Write them in the past tense.
Answer: was, came
Check: The two verbs are identified and the past tense verbs spelt correctly. The sentence is correctly punctuated.

Pupil book answers

Verbs: past and present tense 2

Remember

Lots of **past tense verbs** end with **–ed** but sometimes the word changes in a different way.

I run down the road.   (present tense)
I ran down the road.   (past tense)

The past tense forms should be spelt correctly.

If the children struggle with irregular past tense verbs in speech, start to make and display lists in the classroom for them to refer to.

Try it

1 Write the **verb** from each sentence in the **past tense**.

The boy <u>falls</u> off the slide. ____fell____

I <u>have</u> toast for breakfast. ____had____

I <u>see</u> a snail in the garden. ____saw____

Three fish <u>swim</u> across the lake. ____swam____

The nice lady <u>makes</u> cakes for tea. ____made____

2 Underline the <u>two</u> **present tense verbs** in each sentence. Then rewrite the sentence in the **past tense**.

I <u>take</u> an apple to school and <u>eat</u> it at lunchtime.

I took an apple to school and ate it at lunchtime.

It <u>is</u> hot so Erin <u>wears</u> her shorts.

It was hot so Erin wore her shorts.

The wind <u>blows</u> and the rain <u>comes</u> down.

The wind blew and the rain came down.

Check that the children have identified and changed both verbs, including 'is' in the second question. You may need to recap verbs that are 'being words', which tell you how things *are*.

The past tense forms should be spelt correctly.

Sentence practice

Write a sentence using the **past tense** of the **verb** 'fly'.

The birds flew away.

9

The past tense verb 'flew' should be spelt correctly. Correct any errors [e.g. flewed] so that the children learn the correct form.

The sentence should be correctly punctuated.

Lesson 7 Statements

> Focus understanding the function and grammatical pattern of statements
>
> Key terms sentence, **statement**, verb, capital letter, full stop
>
> Focus text Tigers live in forests in Asia.
> Pandas eat bamboo.
> Elephants are huge.
> The tortoise has a hard shell.
> Whales can hold their breath for a long time.

TEACH

Show the focus text and read the sentences aloud. Discuss the purpose of these sentences [e.g. they tell us something about an animal]. Read each sentence, identifying who or what the sentence is about and underlining it [e.g. Pandas eat bamboo.]. Ask: What does it tell us about them? [e.g. what they eat; what they are like; what they can do]

Explain that these sentences are statements. A statement is a sentence that gives the reader information – it tells us something. It starts with a capital letter and ends with a full stop. In a piece of writing, many of the sentences will be statements. These could be factual [e.g. Elephants are very big.], about ourselves [e.g. I am six.] or about characters in stories [e.g. Cinderella had two sisters.].

Use the statements in the focus text to look at the grammatical pattern: they all start with the name of the animal, followed by a verb. Write over the verbs in colour to make the pattern clear. Explain that this is a common pattern in statements: who or what the sentence is about [the subject] comes first, followed by a verb. Short statements can be extended by adding extra words to the end [e.g. Tigers live in forests in Asia.].

Invite the children to provide some more statements about other animals [e.g. Kangaroos can ...; Giraffes have ...; Camels live ...; Monkeys eat ...] or about themselves [e.g. I live ...; I have ...; I can ...].

EXTEND Look at extending statements by adding words to the beginning [e.g. Most tigers live in ...].

PRACTISE

Pupil book page 10

APPLY

- Ask the children to write five statements to introduce themselves: 'Five important things about me'.
- The children write character profiles giving five statements about a character in a story: 'The five most important things about ...'.
- In other curriculum areas, ask the children to write reports or information texts giving factual statements about the subject [e.g. a place in geography; a person in history; an animal in science].
- Before starting a new topic, the children write statements to show what they already know: 'Things I know about ...'. They then repeat this at the end of a topic, adding new statements to show what they have learnt.

ASSESS

Dictation: Ross is seven years old.
Say: Underline who or what this statement is about. Write two other statements to follow this one.
Answer: e.g. He lives in Westbury. He has a sister and a brother.
Check: The sentences are correctly punctuated.

Pupil book answers

Statements

Remember

A **statement** is a sentence that tells you something. Statements often start with who or what the sentence is about, followed by a **verb**.

<u>Pandas</u> eat bamboo.

Try it

1 Put the words and punctuation in order so they make a **statement**.

in live the sea Whales . <u>Whales live in the sea.</u>

plate Rory a . broke <u>Rory broke a plate.</u>

brown eyes . have I <u>I have brown eyes.</u>

curtains . Kara the opened <u>Kara opened the curtains.</u>

leaves The had tree . no <u>The tree had no leaves.</u>

2 Complete these **statements**.

<u>I can</u> count in twos and tens.

The cook <u>boiled</u> the eggs in a pan of water.

Zebras <u>have black and white stripes and long tails.</u>

<u>Dad put</u> the washing on the line.

<u>The little girl was</u> proud and happy.

Sentence practice

Write a **statement** about what you are wearing.

<u>I am wearing a blue jumper and grey trousers.</u>

10

The statements must start with a capital letter and end with a full stop.

These are just examples. Each sentence should start with a subject [who or what the sentence is about] and verb, and make a grammatically correct statement. Do not accept sentences that are really questions [e.g. Can you count in twos and tens. Are you proud and happy.], as these do not give information and do not follow the subject–verb pattern.

The first word of each statement must start with a capital letter.

The statement must start with a capital letter and end with a full stop.

23

Lesson 8   Questions

> Focus   understanding the function and grammatical pattern of questions
>
> Key terms   sentence, statement, question, full stop, question mark, verb
>
> Focus text   The cow jumped over the moon.
> Why did the cow jump over the moon?
> How did the cow jump over the moon?
> Did the cow jump over the moon?
> Can a cow jump over the moon?

TEACH

Show the first sentence of the focus text. Ask: What type of sentence is this? [a statement – it tells you something] Reveal the other sentences and read them aloud. How are these sentences different from the first one? [e.g. they are questions; they ask something; they end with a question mark]

Explain that questions are another type of sentence. Questions ask us something [e.g. for information] rather than telling us something. They need some sort of response. Questions end with a question mark rather than a full stop.

Use the focus text to look at how questions are formed. The first two questions start with question words [Why, How]. Discuss other question words [e.g. What; When; Who] and invite the children to use them to orally construct other questions about the cow jumping over the moon [e.g. When did the cow jump...? Who saw ...?].

The next two questions start with a verb [Did, Can]. They look like reordered statements: they start with the verb followed by the subject [Did the cow ...? Can a cow ...?]. Invite the children to orally construct other questions with this pattern [e.g. Do cows jump over the moon? Could a cow jump ...?].

EXTEND   Look at other ways of forming questions [e.g. <u>Did you know</u> a cow jumped over the moon? <u>Have you ever seen</u> a cow jump over the moon?].

PRACTISE

Pupil book page 11

APPLY

- The children write questions about pictures and artefacts [e.g. Who are these people? What is this used for?].
- The children write questions to ask a character in a story [e.g. Did you ...? Why did you ...?].
- In other curriculum areas, ask the children to write lists of questions to show: 'What I want to find out'.
- Encourage the use of questions as headings or sub-headings in a non-fiction text [e.g. Where do blackbirds live?].
- The children write letters using statements to give information, and with two questions for the reader to answer.
- Challenge the children to write a poem in the form of questions and answers [e.g. What is red? A postbox is red.].

ASSESS

Dictation: I made these cakes.
Say: Write a question to follow this statement. Any suitable question is acceptable.
Answer: e.g. Would you like to try one?
Check: Both sentences are correctly punctuated.

Pupil book answers

Questions

Remember

A **question** is a sentence that asks something. Questions start with question words or sometimes with **verbs** such as 'Can' and 'Do'. Questions end with a **question mark**.

<u>Where</u> did the cow jump?   <u>Can</u> cows jump?

Try it

1 Add a word to complete each **question**. Then complete the answer.

Question	Statement
<u>What</u> is your name?	My name <u>is Amy Turner.</u>
<u>Who</u> lost a glass slipper?	<u>Cinderella lost</u> a glass slipper.
<u>Is</u> it going to snow?	Yes, <u>it is.</u>
<u>Do</u> you like pizza?	<u>I do / do not</u> like pizza.
<u>Can</u> owls fly?	Yes, <u>owls can fly.</u>

Accept other questions or answers that make grammatical sense [e.g. Would you like pizza? Do owls fly?].

Check to see if the children have remembered to add a full stop where needed.

2 Here is a **statement**. Write some **questions** about it.

Jim went to the shop.

Why <u>did Jim go to the shop?</u>

When <u>did Jim go to the shop?</u>

How <u>did Jim get there?</u>

Did <u>Jim go by bus?</u>

Is <u>Jim still there?</u>

These are just examples. Accept any appropriate questions that make grammatical sense and end with a question mark. Discuss different questions that the children have written.

Sentence practice

Write a **statement** and a **question** about frogs.

<u>Frogs can swim. Can frogs breathe underwater?</u>

11

These are just examples. Accept any statement and question, provided that they make grammatical sense and are punctuated correctly.

Lesson 9 Exclamations

> Focus understanding the function and form of exclamations; revising other types of sentence
>
> Key terms sentence, statement, question, **exclamation**, question mark, exclamation mark
>
> Focus text **Queen:** What's the matter?
> **King:** Someone has stolen my gold coins.
> **Queen:** How terrible! What a shame!

TEACH

Show the focus text. Enjoy reading it together using appropriate intonation. Point out the question mark and exclamation marks and discuss what they tell the reader.

Ask the children to identify the different types of sentence used in the focus text [question, statement, exclamations]. The children will already be familiar with the term 'exclamation mark' but 'exclamation' may be new to them. Underline the exclamations and discuss their purpose. What is special about them? What do they show? [e.g. emotions such as surprise or shock]

Focus on the last line of the focus text. Explain that sentences like these are called exclamations. The words 'what' and 'how' are often used in questions, but exclamations also start with these words. Remind the children that questions ask something and need a reply [e.g. What is the matter? How are you?], while exclamations show emotion [e.g. What a shame! How terrible!]. Invite the children to suggest other exclamations that begin with 'what' or 'how' [e.g. How amazing! What a surprise!].

Explain that interjections such as 'Oh no!' also use exclamation marks but they are not complete sentences. They are short cries that show emotions such as fear, anger, pain, despair, excitement and amazement.

[Note: Exclamation marks are often added to statements or commands to show surprise or strong emotions – e.g. 'It was great!' 'Stop right there!' This tells the reader to use expression when reading the sentence, but it does not change the grammatical pattern of the sentence. They are still statements or commands. This lesson focuses on exclamations that follow the grammatical pattern of starting with 'What' or 'How'.]

EXTEND Discuss the difference between an exclamation starting with 'What' or 'How' and a statement that ends with an exclamation mark.

PRACTISE

Pupil book page 12

APPLY

- Encourage the children to collect exclamations when reading. They can then add pictures to show what emotions they express.
- The children write comic-strip stories using lots of sound effects [e.g. Crash!] and exclamations [e.g. What a great idea!].
- When writing stories, the children use an exclamation to communicate a strong feeling.
- The children write a play script using exclamations to show the feelings of the characters.

ASSESS

Dictation: <u>What a surprise!</u> Dad has won first prize. Does he know yet?
Say: There are three sentences. Underline the exclamation. Check your punctuation.
Check: All three sentences should be correctly punctuated.

Pupil book answers

This lesson focuses on exclamations starting with 'What' or 'How'. These exclamations take their own distinct form, unlike statements or commands that use exclamation marks to show strong feeling.

Grammar 2

Schofield & Sims **Grammar and Punctuation**

Exclamations

Remember

An **exclamation** is a sentence that shows strong feelings. Lots of exclamations start with the words 'What' or 'How'. Exclamations end with an **exclamation mark**.

<u>What</u> a shame!   <u>How</u> terrible!

Try it

1 Some of these sentences are **exclamations** and some are **questions**. Write in the missing **punctuation marks**.

How amazing__!__

How old are you__?__

What a pity__!__

What a surprise__!__

What will you do now__?__

2 Write an **exclamation** to follow each **statement**.

Billy dropped the cake.	What <u>a shame!</u>
I have won a prize.	How <u>exciting!</u>
Let me help you with that.	How <u>kind of you!</u>
I have picked some flowers for you.	How <u>lovely!</u>
All the wolf cubs began to howl.	What <u>a noise!</u>

These are just examples of suitable exclamations. Accept other appropriate exclamations starting with 'What' or 'How' and ending with an exclamation mark. Compare the children's answers.

Do not accept questions, even if they make sense [e.g. What happened?] or if they have been given an exclamation mark [e.g. What happened! How did you do that!]. Remind the children that they are forming exclamations.

Sentence practice

Write a **statement** and an **exclamation** about a game of football.

<u>Our team won 8–0. What a game!</u>

12

These are examples of possible sentences. Exclamations should start with 'What' or 'How' and end with an exclamation mark. Statements should start with a capital letter and end with a full stop.

Lesson 10 Commands

> Focus identifying the function and grammatical pattern of commands
>
> Key terms **command**, sentence, full stop, capital letter, exclamation mark, verb, linking word
>
> Focus text <u>Note for Cinderella</u>
> Clean the grate.
> Make the fire.
> Polish the silver.
> Wash all the dishes.
> Don't stop for a rest.

TEACH

Show the focus text. Read the note aloud in a suitably bossy voice. Discuss who has left it and what its purpose is [e.g. the ugly sisters; to tell Cinderella what to do]. Ask the children if they notice anything special about these sentences [e.g. most start with a verb]. Underline the verbs [e.g. <u>Clean</u> the grate.].

Invite the children to suggest other orders that might be left for Cinderella, expressed in the same way, and add them to the list [e.g. Dust the rooms. Sweep the floor.].

Explain that sentences like these are called commands. Commands instruct or tell someone to do something. They are very direct and use 'bossy' [imperative] verbs, usually at the start of the sentence. These verbs tell us directly what to do [e.g. Stand up. Sit down.].

Point out that the final command starts with 'don't'. Explain that putting the word 'don't', or 'do not', before the verb tells us *not* to do something [e.g. Don't stand up. Do not sit down.].

Discuss how linking words could be added at the start of the commands in the focus text to make a sequence of instructions to Cinderella [e.g. First clean the grate. Next make the fire.].

Explain that commands start with a capital letter and usually end with a full stop. Sometimes we might put an exclamation mark at the end of a command, particularly if it is short, abrupt, or shouted [e.g. Listen to me! Stop!]. However, if it starts with a verb, it is still a command.

EXTEND Change the commands in the note to Cinderella into questions [e.g. Could you clean the grate?]. Discuss how the questions sound more polite, like a request rather than an order.

PRACTISE

Pupil book page 13

APPLY

- Together, use commands to write instructions for classroom routines or to compose a list of classroom rules [e.g. Put your reading bag here. Try your hardest.].
- The children write instructions for making or doing something using a list of numbered commands.
- The children use command verbs [e.g. slice; chop] to write their own recipes.
- The children write instructions for a treasure hunt using commands [e.g. Follow the path ...; Find ...].
- The children write invitations using statements and commands [e.g. Come in fancy dress.].

ASSESS

Dictation: <u>Bring me the book about animals.</u> I want to read it.
Say: Underline the command.
Check: Both sentences are correctly punctuated.

Pupil book answers

Commands

Remember

A **command** is a sentence that instructs or tells someone to do something. Commands often start with a **verb**.

Clean the grate.   Make the fire.

Try it

1 Are these sentences **statements** or **commands?** Write 'statement' or 'command'.

Stop doing that.   command

The car made a terrible noise.   statement

Don't let the dog off its lead.   command

Rowan plays with the hamster.   statement

Plants need water to grow.   statement

2 Complete these **commands** with a suitable **verb**.

_____Throw_____ the dice to start the game.

_____Get_____ the hammer from the shed.

Please _____feed_____ the fish on Monday.

Don't _____drop_____ the eggs on the floor.

_____Tell_____ me a story before I go to bed.

> Other verbs could be used. The verbs should be imperative forms with no subject [e.g. 'Throw' rather than 'You throw'].
>
> Where the verb is the first word in the sentence, it should begin with a capital letter. If another word precedes it, there should be no capital letter.

Sentence practice

Mum wants Joe to tidy his bedroom. Write <u>two</u> suitable **commands**.

Pick up the books. Put the toys in the toy box.

_____

13

These are examples of suitable commands. Both sentences should use imperative verbs, begin with capital letters and end with full stops.

Revision 1 answers

These pages revise content from **Grammar 1**. Some areas have not been covered as yet in this book, so it is important to see if the children have retained knowledge and understanding. The focus of each activity is given to help identify areas where the children might need further revision.

Focus: capital letters for names

This has been reinforced in Section 1. There will be further coverage of this topic in Section 3, as part of the discussion of proper nouns.

In the fourth sentence 'Does' should not be underlined as it already has a capital letter.

Revision 1

1 Underline the <u>three</u> words in each sentence that need a **capital letter**.

<u>sam</u> and <u>lucy</u> met <u>sita</u> at the corner shop.

<u>i</u> think <u>josh</u> was going to <u>spain</u> for his holiday.

<u>gran</u> and <u>grandad</u> always go shopping on <u>monday</u> morning.

Does <u>harry</u> live in <u>hobbs</u> <u>lane</u>?

Focus: punctuating sentences with full stops, question marks or exclamation marks

This also reviews the four sentence types introduced in Section 1.

2 Add the **punctuation mark** needed to complete these sentences.

Can I come and play_<u> ? </u>

Put the paper in the printer_<u> . </u>

Today it rained all day_<u> . </u>

What a shock_<u> ! </u>

Focus: forming sentences

This activity reminds the children to reread sentences they have written, to check that they are complete.

It also draws on the children's knowledge of using 'and' in sentences and emphasises the importance of verbs in forming sentences.

3 Each sentence has a word missing. Write the full **sentence** so it makes sense.

He put on his coat went outside.

<u>He put on his coat and went outside.</u>

Once upon a time there a little goat.

<u>Once upon a time there was a little goat.</u>

4 Choose the correct word, **'and'**, **'then'** or **'finally'**, to complete each sentence. Write it in the space.

First wash your face. <u>   Then   </u> get dressed.

Have some toast <u>   and   </u> drink your milk.

<u>   Finally   </u>, brush your teeth <u>   and   </u> put on your coat.

14

Focus: sequencing and linking sentences; using 'and' to join words or clauses

This activity checks that the children know to use 'and' to join two ideas *within* a sentence, and 'then' to link separate sentences.

'Then' must start with a capital letter; 'and' must be lower case.

Schofield & Sims **Grammar and Punctuation**

Grammar 2

5 Write the **plural** of these words.

gate	_gates_	tree	_trees_
bench	_benches_	owl	_owls_
railing	_railings_	flower	_flowers_
bush	_bushes_	fox	_foxes_

Focus: using the regular plural noun suffixes –s or –es

This activity checks that the children recognise and understand the word 'plural' and know that –s and –es are the suffixes used to form regular plurals. Plurals will be revisited in Section 3.

The plural words must be spelt correctly.

6 Choose the correct word to complete each sentence. Write it in the space.

The _painter_ dropped his brush.   (painting painter painted)

He is _picking_ up the litter.   (picking picker picked)

They _waited_ for hours.   (waiting waiter waited)

I _played_ football yesterday.   (playing player played)

Focus: verb endings

This has been reinforced in Section 1, through work on verbs and tense.

7 Add **un–** to these **verbs**.

_un_ load   _un_ pack   _un_ tie

Now write a **sentence** using each new verb you have made.

I saw the workers unload the lorry.

I helped Mum unpack the shopping.

I can't untie my laces.

Focus: how the prefix un– changes the meaning of verbs

This has not been covered in this book, so check that the children understand that adding un– to verbs means 'un-doing'.

The sentences shown are just examples but the children should use the words in a suitable context. The sentences should be correctly punctuated.

8 Rewrite each question as a **command**.

Could you get me a drink of water?

Get me a drink of water.

Do you want to come and play at my house?

Come and play at my house.

15

Focus: identifying the function and grammatical pattern of commands

The verb should be an imperative form with the subject [e.g. *not* You get/You could get]. Check that the question mark has been replaced with a full stop.

Writing task 1: Analysis sheet

Tick the circles to show amount of evidence found in writing:
1 No evidence
2 Some evidence
3 Clear evidence

Pupil name: _____

Date: _____

Assessing punctuation

The writing sample demonstrates:	Evidence		
capital letters used at the beginning of sentences.	1	2	3
sentence boundaries recognised and demarcated with full stops.	1	2	3
question marks and exclamation marks used when required.	1	2	3
capital letters used for 'I', names of people and places, and days of the week.	1	2	3

Assessing grammar and sentence structure

The writing sample demonstrates:	Evidence		
grammatically correct sentences.	1	2	3
correct use of the conjunctions 'and', 'but', 'or' to form longer sentences.	1	2	3
different sentence types [e.g. statements about the events; exclamations to show excitement – What a surprise!; questions for the reader].	1	2	3
correct use of tense [past tense to recount what happened; using past tense forms of regular –ed and irregular verbs].	1	2	3
additional detail [e.g. using adjectives to describe].	1	2	3
sentences sequenced to form a logical account [e.g. Then ...; Next ...].	1	2	3

Key target: _____

From: **Grammar 2 Teacher's Guide** © *Schofield & Sims Ltd, 2017. This page may be photocopied after purchase.*

Writing task 1: Pupil checklist

Name: _____   Date: _____

Reread what you have written to check that it makes sense. Tick the circle if you have correctly used the punctuation or grammar feature in your writing.

Punctuation

◯ I have used capital letters at the beginning of sentences.

◯ I have used full stops at the end of sentences.

◯ I have used a question mark or exclamation mark if it is needed.

◯ I have used capital letters for 'I', names of people and places, and days of the week.

Grammar and sentences

◯ I have written in sentences and they make sense.

◯ I have used different sentence types (for example, statements, an exclamation or a question).

◯ I have used 'and', 'but', 'or' to make some longer sentences.

◯ I have used past tense verbs to say what happened.

◯ I have added some detail by using describing words.

◯ I have used words such as 'Then, 'Next' to sequence and link what happened.

Teacher feedback

My key target: _____

_____

*From: **Grammar 2 Teacher's Guide** © Schofield & Sims Ltd, 2017. This page may be photocopied after purchase.*

Lesson 11   Nouns and noun phrases

> Focus   identifying nouns and noun phrases in sentences
>
> Key terms   **noun, noun phrase**
>
> Focus text   The dog barked at the bus and made a man fall off his bike.
> Then the dog chased a police car past the bank and the
> post office and round the corner.

TEACH

Show the focus text. Read it aloud and ask the children to picture the events. Ask: Where do you picture the events happening – in a park, in the street, in a school? Why? Discuss how the highlighted words help us to picture the events by naming things in the scene.

Explain that the highlighted words are called nouns: words that name somebody [e.g. man] or something [e.g. bike]. Use the focus text to show that the words 'the' or 'a' are often used before a noun. Point out that this is a good way of deciding if a word is a noun – for example, we can say 'the'/'a bike', so we know 'bike' is a noun. [Note: Different types of noun are introduced in Lesson 26 and later in the programme.]

Explain that, when the words 'the' or 'a' are placed before a noun, this makes a noun phrase. A noun phrase is made up of the noun and any words that go with it. Ask the children to identify the noun phrases in the focus text [the dog, the bus, a man, his bike, a police car, the bank, the post office, the corner]. Underline them.

Point out that, in the second sentence, some of the noun phrases are three words long [e.g. a police car]. This is because two nouns are used together to name something [a police car – not just a car].

Create new sentences, putting the troublesome dog in a different setting [e.g. at the seaside]. Ask the children to suggest suitable nouns for the new setting and to use these in a sentence [e.g. The dog barked at the seagull and made the man fall off his surfboard.].

EXTEND   Add words after the noun to expand a noun phrase [e.g. The dog <u>on the beach</u> …].
[Note: This will be covered in more detail in Lesson 29.]

PRACTISE

Pupil book page 18

APPLY

- Reinforce the term 'noun' by naming and labelling items in the classroom and on displays.
- In other subject areas, discuss and display nouns linked to a theme and encourage the children to use these in writing [e.g. a habitat in science; the geographical features of a location].
- In other subjects, the children label diagrams using nouns [e.g. parts of the body; parts of plants].
- The children write a list of nouns associated with the setting of a story and then use them in the story.
- Encourage the careful choice of nouns to help give a clear picture [e.g. chemist rather than shop].

ASSESS

Dictation: The <u>monkey</u> sat in the <u>tree</u> and watched the <u>snake</u>.
Say: Underline the three nouns. Now write the sentence with three different nouns.
Answer: e.g. The cat sat in the garden and watched the bird.
Check: The correct nouns are underlined. The new sentence is correctly punctuated and the correct past tense –ed ending on the verb 'watched' is used.

Pupil book answers

Nouns and noun phrases

Remember

Nouns are words that name things, such as 'man', 'dog' or 'bus'.

The dog barked at the bus.

A **noun phrase** is made up of the noun and any other words that go with it.

The dog chased a police car.

Only the three words shown should be underlined in each sentence. Check that the children have identified nouns even if they are not preceded by 'the' or 'a' [e.g. purse; ears]. Point out that they could be 'a purse', 'the ears'.

Try it

1 Underline all the **nouns** in these sentences.

The <u>waiter</u> carried the <u>tray</u> to the <u>table</u>.

The <u>lady</u> counted the <u>money</u> in her <u>purse</u>.

The <u>man</u> sat on a <u>bench</u> in the <u>park</u> and waited.

The little <u>boy</u> dropped the <u>sweets</u> on the <u>floor</u>.

The <u>elephant</u> has a <u>trunk</u> and large <u>ears</u>.

This activity asks the children to underline the nouns, so strictly speaking the words 'the' or 'a' should not be underlined as these form part of a noun phrase. However, you may want to explain this to the children rather than mark it as incorrect.

2 Complete each sentence using <u>two</u> suitable **nouns**.

Dad is digging a _____hole_____ in the _____garden_____ .

Emma rode her _____bike_____ round the _____playground_____ .

The girl put the _____book_____ on the _____shelf_____ .

The bird sat on the _____branch_____ of a _____tree_____ .

The fox sat by the _____fence_____ watching the _____hens_____ .

These are examples of suitable nouns. Any nouns that make sense in the context of the sentence are correct. Compare the children's answers to see the effect of different choices.

Sentence practice

Write a sentence about a cat in the garden. Use at least <u>three</u> **nouns**.

The cat found a bird in the garden.

18

This is an example of a possible sentence. You could ask the children to underline the nouns they use. Compare the children's sentences.

Check that the sentence is correctly punctuated.

Lesson 12 Adjectives

Focus using adjectives to describe or specify nouns

Key terms noun, noun phrase, **adjective**

Focus text **Once there was a farmer who lived in a cottage by a stream.**
Once there was a poor farmer who lived in a rundown cottage
by a little stream.

TEACH

Show the first sentence of the focus text and read it aloud. Explain that this is the start of a story. Discuss what it tells us about the character and the setting of the story. Ask the children to identify the three nouns and noun phrases in the sentence [a farmer, a cottage, a stream].

Show the second sentence and read it aloud. Discuss why this version is better [e.g. because the highlighted 'describing words' tell us more about the farmer, the cottage and the stream]. Discuss why it might be important to know that the farmer was poor and that he lived in a rundown cottage.

Explain that the highlighted words are called adjectives: words that describe or tell us more about a noun. Adjectives help to give a better picture of the noun [e.g. a rundown cottage] or add important details [e.g. a poor farmer]. Adjectives can also show which noun is being talked about [e.g. there might be a little stream and a big stream].

Underline the noun phrases in the second sentence of the focus text [a poor farmer, a rundown cottage, a little stream]. Discuss how the adjective is placed before the noun to become part of the noun phrase. Invite the children to suggest other adjectives to fit the noun phrases [e.g. the lonely/rich farmer; a smart/tiny cottage].

EXTEND Show that adjectives can be placed *after* the noun, using the verb 'is'/'was' [e.g. the farmer was poor].

PRACTISE

Pupil book page 19

APPLY

- Look for adjectives in story titles [e.g. The Enormous Turnip; The Magic Paintbrush]. Invite the children to make up their own titles using different adjectives [e.g. The Gigantic Paintbrush].
- In stories, the children use adjectives to describe characters and settings.
- The children write about interesting objects or imaginary creatures, choosing adjectives carefully.
- Collect 'amazing adjectives' from stories and poems for the children to use in their own writing.
- In non-fiction texts, discuss how adjectives are used to describe and specify [e.g. it has small feet; fold the blue paper in half].
- Ask the children to highlight the adjectives they use in a piece of writing. Discuss why the adjectives were used. Were they well chosen? Is there a better adjective?
- In pairs, ask the children to reread a piece of writing to decide where an adjective could be added to improve it.

ASSESS

Dictation: The girl found a strange box hidden in the cave.
Say: Underline the adjective in this sentence. Add an adjective to describe another noun in the sentence.
Answer: The second adjective could be added to 'girl' or 'cave' [e.g. 'The young girl' or 'the dark cave'].

Pupil book answers

Adjectives

Remember

An **adjective** is a word that tells you more about a **noun**.
You use adjectives to describe things or to add important details about nouns.

Once there was a poor <u>farmer</u> who lived in a rundown <u>cottage</u>.

Try it

1　Underline all the **adjectives** in these sentences.

The <u>angry</u> bees buzzed around the tree.

The king wore his <u>new</u> crown to the party.

The pirate had a parrot with <u>green</u> feathers.

She sailed across the sea to a <u>strange</u> land.

The <u>little</u> mouse hid in the <u>long</u> grass.

Only the words shown should be underlined. You could ask the children which noun each one describes.

Check that the children have identified both adjectives in the fifth sentence.

2　Complete each sentence by adding a suitable **adjective** to the nouns in **bold**.

The _____fierce_____ **wolf** showed his _____sharp_____ **teeth**.

My cat Felix is a _____crafty_____ **cat** and a _____clever_____ **cat**.

The giant lived in a _____huge_____ **house** with a _____creaky_____ **door**.

The _____foamy_____ **waves** crashed on to the _____grey_____ **rocks**.

The boy took the _____grassy_____ **path** into the _____dark_____ **woods**.

These are examples of suitable adjectives. Any adjective that makes sense in the context of the sentence is acceptable but you could use this activity to focus on choosing adjectives carefully or using more interesting words. Compare the children's choices. Which is the 'best' choice? Why?

Sentence practice

Write a sentence about a clown using <u>two</u> or more **adjectives**.

The clown wore a red bow tie and baggy trousers.

19

This is an example of a suitable sentence. At this stage the children may choose simple adjectives, but they should still be encouraged to make careful choices.

Lesson 13 Adjectives with suffixes –ful, –less

> Focus forming adjectives using suffixes such as –ful, –less, –y
>
> Key terms adjective, **suffix**, noun
>
> Focus text **Prince Herman was a** careful **prince.**
> **Prince Edgar was a** careless **prince.**

TEACH

Show the focus text. Read aloud the two sentences. Discuss how the two princes are different and which words make this clear [careful, careless]. Ask: What might a careful prince do? What about a careless prince? Establish the different meanings of these two words [e.g. full of care; without care].

Discuss what type of word is highlighted [adjectives: they tell us more about the noun – the prince]. Ask the children what they notice about the two adjectives [they both begin with the word 'care' but they have different endings, –ful and –less].

Explain that the endings –ful and –less are called suffixes. A suffix is a group of letters added on to the end of a word to make a new word with a different meaning. For example, –ful and –less are added to words to make adjectives, which can be used to describe people or things. Establish that –ful means 'full of'; –less means 'without'.

Use two or three other words [e.g. hope; power; fear] in the focus text to replace 'care'. Discuss the meaning of the new words you make [e.g. hopeful/hopeless; powerful/powerless; fearful/fearless]. Ask the children to think of other adjectives with these suffixes. You may wish to point out that –ful and –less cannot always be added to the same word [e.g. 'forgetful' is a word but 'forgetless' is not].

Discuss other familiar suffixes used to form adjectives, such as the suffix –y [e.g. a lucky/sleepy/cheeky/greedy prince].

EXTEND Look at other suffixes used to form adjectives, such as –ish [e.g. foolish] and –en [e.g. wooden].

PRACTISE

Pupil book page 20

APPLY

- The children write stories about characters [e.g. Fearless Fergus; Powerful Percy; Forgetful Felix] to show the meaning of the words. Alternatively, they write what happens when two contrasting characters meet [e.g. Careful Colin and Careless Cora].
- When reading stories or poems together, collect adjectives ending with –ful or –less [e.g. beautiful; pitiful; restless]. Display these in the classroom and encourage the children to use them when writing.
- In other subjects, draw attention to adjectives formed by adding suffixes [e.g. in design and technology or cooking – useful; bendy; tasteless].
- Challenge the children to use at least one adjective ending with –ful or –less when writing a story or description.

ASSESS

Dictation: My granny is forget but she is a wonder cook.
Say: Two words in this sentence need a suffix. Underline the words and write them correctly.
Answer: My granny is forgetful but she is a wonderful cook.

Pupil book answers

Adjectives with suffixes –ful, –less

Remember

Some **adjectives** are made by adding the **suffixes –ful** or **–less** to a word.

careful   Prince Herman was a careful man.
careless   Prince Edgar was a careless man.

Try it

1   Use the **suffix –ful** or **–less** to make each word into an **adjective**. Write the adjective.

wonder	wonderful	peace	peaceful
forget	forgetful	home	homeless
speech	speechless	hate	hateful
spot	spotless	wish	wishful

> The adjectives should be spelt correctly – both root word and suffix [a common error is to spell the –ful suffix 'full'].

2   Complete each sentence by making an **adjective** ending with **–ful** or **–less**.

The doctor said a broken arm can be pain_ful_ .

A moth is a harm_less_ insect.

The small boy was power_less_ against the mighty dragon.

The flowers in the garden were bright and colour_ful_ .

The book about plants was very help_ful_ and interesting.

> Both suffixes can be added to these words but the context of the sentence means that only one word is appropriate. The activity checks the children's understanding of the meaning of the adjectives formed by adding the suffixes –ful or –less.

Sentence practice

Add the **suffixes –ful** and **–less** to the word 'use'. Write **two** sentences, one for each of the **adjectives** you make.

A rubber is useful if you make a mistake.

Our old toaster was useless.

> These are just examples. The sentences should show the different meaning of the adjectives. The adjectives should be spelt correctly.

20

Lesson 14 **Adjectives with suffixes –er, –est**

Focus using the suffixes –er, –est in adjectives

Key terms adjective, suffix

Focus text George the giant was strong.
Jude the giant was stronger.
Jed was the strongest giant of all.

TEACH

Show the focus text and read it aloud. Discuss what it tells us about the three giants. Establish that it is comparing the three giants, saying which is stronger and which the strongest. Ask the children what they notice about the highlighted words [e.g. they are adjectives; they describe or tell us more about the giants; they use the word 'strong'; the words have the suffixes –er and –est].

Explain that words such as 'stronger' and 'strongest' are a special sort of adjective that we use to compare things or describe differences. These special adjectives are formed by adding the suffixes –er and –est to an adjective. Adjectives with –er [comparative adjectives] *compare* two things; adjectives with –est [superlative adjectives] say which is the *most* ... [Note: The children do not need to know the terms 'comparative' and 'superlative' at this stage, just how the words are used.]

Introduce a different adjective into the first sentence [e.g. George the giant was tall/kind/brave.]. Invite the children to compare the three giants again, adding –er and –est to the new word [e.g. taller, tallest].

Use the focus text to point out that when using adjectives with –est we add the word 'the' before the adjective [e.g. <u>the</u> strongest; <u>the</u> kindest; <u>the</u> tallest; <u>the</u> bravest]. Explain that this is because there can only be one person or thing that is the *most* ...

EXTEND Introduce unusual comparatives and superlatives [e.g. George is good, Jude is better, Jed is the best – *not* 'gooder', 'goodest'] or longer words that use 'more' and 'most' rather than –er and –est [e.g. powerful, more powerful, most powerful].

PRACTISE

Pupil book page 21

APPLY

- The children write boasts [e.g. for a giant or a boastful character], using adjectives ending with –er and –est [e.g. No-one is braver than me. I am the tallest giant in the world.].
- In other subjects, focus on the use of –er and –est when making comparisons, such as weather patterns in geography [e.g. colder; warmer; wetter; sunnier]; materials in design and technology [e.g. softer; stronger; stiffer; smoother; rougher; lighter]; sounds or movements in science [e.g. louder; softer; higher; lower; faster; slower; the fastest] or measurements in mathematics [e.g. heavier; lighter].
- The children use comparative and superlative adjectives to write about contrasting characters in stories [e.g. The hare is the fastest animal. The tortoise is slower but wiser.].

ASSESS

Dictation: The cross driver was stuck behind a <u>slower</u> car.
Say: Underline the adjective that compares two things. [Note: 'Cross' is an adjective but is not comparing anything here; 'driver' has the suffix –er but is not an adjective.]

Pupil book answers

Adjectives with suffixes –er, –est

Remember

You can use **adjectives** to compare things by adding the **suffixes –er** or **–est**.

George was strong. Jude was stronger. Jed was the strongest of all.

The adjectives should be spelt correctly, including those that require a change to the spelling [braver, bravest; happier, happiest]. Discuss these changes in spelling if necessary: words ending with an 'e' drop the 'e' when adding –er, –est; in words ending with a 'y', the 'y' changes to 'i' when adding –er, –est.

Try it

1 Add the **suffixes –er** and **–est** to these **adjectives**. Write the new adjectives.

soft	softer	softest
slow	slower	slowest
loud	louder	loudest
brave	braver	bravest
happy	happier	happiest

2 Choose the correct word to complete each sentence. Write it in the space.

He is the ___richest___ man in all the land. (rich richer richest)

Rosie is ___older___ than her sister. (old older oldest)

Merlin was the ___wisest___ wizard of all. (wise wiser wisest)

A car is ___quicker___ than a bike. (quick quicker quickest)

My room is ___smaller___ than yours. (small smaller smallest)

If necessary, remind the children that 'the' comes before the –est form of the word.

Sentence practice

Add the **suffixes –er** and **–est** to the word 'fast'. Write two sentences, one for each of the **adjectives** you make.

Fox was faster than the ducks and sheep. He was the fastest thing on four legs.

21

This is just an example of how the words 'faster' and 'fastest' might be used in sentences. Check that the word 'fastest' is preceded by 'the'.

Both sentences should be correctly punctuated.

Lesson 15   Joining words: 'when', 'because'

> Focus   introducing the subordinating conjunctions 'when', 'because'
>
> Key terms   sentence, joining word
>
> Focus text   The lion sniffed the air and he licked his lips.
> The lion sniffed the air because he could smell food.
> The lion sniffed the air when he woke up.

TEACH

Show the first sentence of the focus text. Read it aloud, miming what the lion does. Ask the children why they think he did these things [e.g. he was hungry; he could smell food]. Reveal and read the second sentence. Explain that this sentence tells us why he sniffed the air. Reveal the third sentence and read it aloud. Discuss what this sentence tells us [*when* he sniffed the air].

Discuss how the three sentences are similar and different [e.g. different words in place of 'and'; different endings giving different information]. Ask: Why are the highlighted words used? What do they do? [e.g. they join together two ideas]

Explain that the words 'when' and 'because' are joining words: they join together two ideas in one sentence. We can use these words to add more information to an existing sentence, as in the focus text. [Note: The technical term for joining words is 'conjunction'. The children do not need to know this term yet, so they are called joining words in this book. You can use 'conjunction' if you wish.]

Use the focus text to discuss what sort of extra information is added after 'because' and 'when' [e.g. 'because' gives a reason – it answers the question 'Why?'; 'when' tells us the point at which something happened – it answers the question 'When?']. Invite the children to suggest alternative endings for the second and third sentences [e.g. ... because he was hungry; ... when he went into the cave].

EXTEND   Explain that 'because' and 'when' add more detail about the main idea in a sentence [subordinating conjunction], while 'and' joins two separate or equal ideas [co-ordinating conjunction] – as in the first sentence.

PRACTISE

Pupil book page 22

APPLY

- Ask the children to use 'because' to answer 'why' questions about stories [e.g. Why did Jack climb the beanstalk?] or 'why' questions in other subject areas [e.g. Why are windows made from glass?].
- The children write explanations that explain how and why things happen, giving reasons [e.g. The water freezes because it is cold. The snow melts when the sun comes out.].
- Encourage the children to use 'because' to give reasons for choices [e.g. My favourite book/toy/game/ food is ... because ...].
- Together, look at how 'when' and 'because' are used in stories [e.g. to link events or show character].
- The children use conjunctions when writing about personal experiences or events in history [e.g. The fire spread quickly because ...; The people ran when ...].

ASSESS

Dictation: The baby started to cry. He was hungry.

Say: Write these two sentences as one sentence using a joining word.

Answer: The baby started to cry when/because he was hungry.

Check: The sentences are correctly punctuated.

Pupil book answers

Joining words: 'when', 'because'

Remember

The words '**when**' and '**because**' are **joining words**.
They join together two ideas in one sentence.
They help to give more information in a sentence.

The lion sniffed the air.
The lion sniffed the air because he could smell food.
The lion sniffed the air when he woke up.

Try it

1 Choose the best **joining word**, '**because**' or '**when**', to complete each sentence.

The teacher was tired _____when_____ she got home.

I am shivering ____because____ I am cold.

Amaya yawned _____when_____ she woke up.

I like fruit ____because____ it is good for you.

Dad won first prize ____because____ his cake was the best.

2 Complete these sentences.

The tiger roared when _he saw the hunter._

The king was happy because _he had lots of money._

William laughed when _the clown fell over._

She did not sleep because _she was so excited._

He was reading his book when _there was a knock at the door._

Sentence practice

Write a sentence about a melting ice cream. Use one of the **joining words** '**because**' or '**when**'.

My ice cream started to melt because it was hot in the sun.

These are just examples. The sentences should make sense and follow on logically from the conjunction, giving a suitable reason or event. Compare different sentences that the children have written.

Check that sentences are correctly punctuated with a full stop at the end and no capital letter after the conjunction.

This is an example of a possible sentence. The sentence should be correctly punctuated as one sentence, with no capital letter at the start of 'because' or 'when'.

22

Lesson 16 Joining words: 'if', 'that'

Focus   using the subordinating conjunctions 'if', 'that' to add more to a sentence

Key terms   sentence, joining word

Focus text   Dad said my sunflower will grow if I water it every day.
I hope that my sunflower will grow really tall.

TEACH

Show the focus text, revealing just the first part of each sentence up to the conjunction [if, that]. Read the start of the first sentence and invite the children to suggest how it might continue – '... if ... what?'. Then reveal the complete sentence. Do the same with the second sentence [up to 'that'], discussing what the writer might hope, before revealing the complete sentence.

Explain that the words 'that' and 'if', like 'because' and 'when', are joining words. They join together two ideas to make one sentence. They are used to add more detail about the main idea in a sentence.

Use the focus text to discuss how the words 'if' and 'that' can be used in a sentence. So, for example, the first sentence tells us that something will happen [the sunflower will grow], but only if something else happens [I water it]. In the second sentence, the first part of the sentence tells us 'I hope' and the second part of the sentence explains what that hope is [that the sunflower will grow really tall].

Explain that the added part of the sentence that begins with the joining word does not make sense on its own. It needs the first, main part of the sentence. Demonstrate this using the focus text [e.g. 'that my sunflower will grow really tall' does not make sense without 'I hope'].

Introduce a different subject [e.g. my birthday party] and invite the children to orally compose new sentences using those in the focus text as models [e.g. Dad said I can have a party if ...; I hope that ...].

EXTEND   Introduce other subordinating conjunctions [e.g. while; so], and explain how they are used.

PRACTISE

Pupil book page 23

APPLY

- The children write descriptive sentences or a list poem using a repeated sentence opener [e.g. It was so quiet that ...; I would jump for joy if ...].
- Display examples of sentences from reading to show how joining words are used. Use these as models for the children to write their own sentences.
- Use 'if' to explore key points in stories [e.g. Cinderella will be happy if ...].
- The children write sentences based on 'This is the house that Jack built'.
- Challenge the children to use two or three different joining words when they are writing a story. Ask them to highlight the joining words used.

ASSESS

Dictation: Mum said <u>that</u> I will need my coat <u>if</u> it gets cold.
Say: Underline the two joining words in this sentence.
Check: The sentence is correctly punctuated.

Pupil book answers

Joining words: 'if', 'that'

Remember

The words 'if' and 'that' are **joining words**. They join together two ideas in one sentence. They help to add more detail about the main idea in a sentence.

My sunflower will grow if I water it every day.
I hope that it will grow really tall.

Try it

1 Complete each sentence using the **joining word** 'if' or 'that'.

I would keep very still ____if____ I saw a snake.

Megan told me ____that____ I was in the team.

My dog starts to bark ____if____ it hears a noise.

I like stories ____if____ they are funny.

The man boasted ____that____ he was clever.

2 Complete these sentences.

I will give you a bag of gold if you help me.

The boy was so frightened that he ran away.

I will help if you have a problem.

I am glad that you are coming to play.

The man promised that he would come back.

These are just examples. The sentences must make sense and be grammatically correct. Compare the children's answers.

The sentences should be correctly punctuated with a full stop at the end. There should be no capital letter after the conjunction.

Sentence practice

Complete this sentence. Use one of the **joining words** 'that' or 'if'.

I feel sad that you are leaving.

23

This is just an example of a possible sentence. Either 'if' or 'that' could be used [e.g. I feel sad if I lose a game.]. Compare the different ways in which the children complete the sentence.

Lesson 17 Compound nouns

> Focus forming compound nouns
>
> Key terms noun, **compound noun**
>
> Focus text As the daylight began to fade, a bluebird and a grasshopper met on the footpath near the old windmill.

TEACH

Show the focus text. Discuss what sort of story it might be, where it takes place and who the characters are [e.g. animal characters suggest it might be a traditional story or a fable].

Ask the children to identify the five nouns in the sentence – the words that name things [daylight, bluebird, grasshopper, footpath, windmill]. Underline the nouns. Ask the children if they notice anything special about these nouns [e.g. they are all made up of two shorter words].

Explain that nouns like these are called compound nouns: they are made up of two shorter words that are pushed together to form one new longer word. Point out that there is no space between the two shorter words, and that this can be important for understanding meaning [e.g. 'a bluebird' – the name of a particular type of bird – is different from 'a blue bird' – any blue bird].

Discuss the meaning of the compound nouns in the focus text and how they are formed, noting that the formation of a compound noun and its meaning are closely related [e.g. 'bluebird' names a type of bird that is blue; 'footpath' names a path used by feet; 'daylight' names the light during the day].

Explain that many nouns are formed in this way. Ask the children if they can suggest any others. Check that the children's suggestions are all compound nouns, rather than words that split into two smaller nouns but do not have a meaning related to them [e.g. car-pet], or words that split into two smaller parts but not two stand-alone words [e.g. wig-wam]. These are not compound nouns.

EXTEND Explore the history of compound nouns such as 'cupboard' and 'cloakroom'.

PRACTISE

Pupil book page 24

APPLY

- Identify compound nouns linked to different topics, themes or settings [e.g. the seaside – starfish; surfboard; deckchair; seagull; seaweed; lighthouse].
- Discuss compound nouns in other subjects. These could be significant words in history [e.g. gunpowder] or names of insects or flowers in science [e.g. grasshopper; bluebell].
- The children make a glossary or an ABC book of compound nouns, including pictures and definitions.
- Together, think of some ideas for new compound nouns. What would they mean? Write definitions [e.g. a 'moonpath' – a path on the moon].

ASSESS

Dictation: We went to the fairground. We rode on the big wheel and I had some popcorn.
Say: There is a compound noun in each sentence. Underline it.
Check: The compound nouns are identified and written as one word. Check that both sentences are demarcated with capital letters and full stops.

Pupil book answers

Compound nouns

Remember

A **compound noun** is made up of two words pushed together. The two words together make one new noun.

footpath   daylight   bluebird

Try it

1 Add another word to make a **compound noun**.

play _time_   _green_ house

goal _post_   _wheel_ chair

star _light_   _hand_ stand

head _band_   _net_ ball

snow _man_   _pan_ cake

2 Complete the **compound nouns** so that each sentence makes sense.

On his seventh birth _day_ Christopher took his new _skate_ board to the play _ground_ .

Hannah left her hand _bag_ at the _super_ market check _out_ .

In the biggest bed _room_ , there was a purple _book_ case next to the fire _place_ .

A sign _post_ pointed to the water _fall_ , where we saw a beautiful rain _bow_ .

Sentence practice

Write a sentence about a trip to the beach, using **three** or more **compound nouns**.

I found a starfish and some seaweed at the seaside.

24

Just some of the possible answers are shown here. Many others are possible [e.g. playground; goalkeeper; starfish; headlight; snowball; lighthouse; armchair; headstand; football; cheesecake]. This is a good exercise for comparing the children's answers.

Check that the words are compound nouns, not two separate nouns [e.g. rugby ball; birthday cake; doll's house]. Compound nouns should be written with no space between the two parts.

There are other possible answers for some questions [e.g. suitcase rather than bookcase].

Check that the compound nouns are written correctly with no space.

This is an example of a possible answer. Check that the words are compound nouns and that they are written correctly with no space.

Lesson 18 Commas in lists

Focus using commas to separate items in a list

Key terms sentence, punctuation mark, **comma**, noun, adjective, verb

Focus text The little elephant squirted water over the lion, the monkey, the rhino and the snake.
The animals were cold, wet and very angry.

TEACH

Show the focus text. Read the first sentence aloud. Ask: How many animals did elephant squirt water over? Read the sentence together, pausing and counting each animal on your fingers. Underline each animal in the list. Ask the children if they can name the punctuation mark used after 'lion' and 'monkey' [comma].

Read the second sentence. Ask: How many adjectives are used to describe the animals? Count and underline them as before. Ask: What punctuation mark is used after 'cold'? Why? [e.g. to show a pause]

Explain that sometimes we write sentences with lists of three or more items. These items are often nouns, as in the first sentence, but they can also be adjectives, as in the second sentence, or even verbs. In sentences like these, commas are used to clearly separate the items in the list.

Use the focus text to look at the position of the commas. Show that a comma is placed after each noun or adjective until the last two, when 'and' is used instead. Remind the children that if there were only two nouns or adjectives, we would use 'and' [e.g. The water went over the lion and the snake.].

Invite the children to compose another sentence about the little elephant with a different list of animals or one using a list of verbs to show what happened next [e.g. The animals growled, grumbled, snorted and hissed at the elephant.]. Discuss where the commas should go and when to use 'and'. Write the sentence, reinforcing that there should be no comma before 'and'.

EXTEND Write sentences with lists of noun phrases [e.g. … the angry lion, the furious rhino …].

PRACTISE

Pupil book page 25

APPLY

- In other subjects, look for opportunities for the children to write sentences with lists [e.g. in science – 'In the woodland, we saw …'; 'We use wood to make …'; 'Rabbits eat …'; in geography – 'The village has …' or in design and technology – 'You will need …'; 'It is made from …'].
- In pairs, the children take it in turns to add nouns to a written sentence [e.g. On the farm, I saw …].
- The children write sentences with lists based on cumulative stories [e.g. Henny Penny met Goosey Lucy, Ducky Lucky …; The old man pulled, the old woman pulled, the big dog pulled …].
- The children write sentences listing the contents of an imaginary suitcase.
- When writing a story or account, challenge the children to include a sentence with a list [e.g. We had a picnic with sandwiches, crisps, fruit and bottles of water.].

ASSESS

Dictation: I go to school on Monday, Tuesday, Wednesday, Thursday and Friday.
Say: Check your punctuation.
Check: The sentence is correctly punctuated, with no comma after Thursday. The days of the week begin with capital letters and are spelt correctly.

Pupil book answers

Commas in lists

Remember

You use **commas** to separate items in a list. With the last two items, you use '**and**' instead of a comma.

The little elephant squirted water over the lion, the monkey, the rhino and the snake.

Try it

1 Add the missing **commas** to each sentence.

Mum makes plum, strawberry and blackberry jam.

Blackbirds eat insects, worms and berries.

We saw ducks, geese, swans and moorhens on the river.

You need paper, scissors, glue, paints and a big box.

The leaves were red, yellow, orange and brown.

> Make sure there is no comma before 'and'.

2 Add <u>three</u> more items to each list. Use the correct **punctuation**.

The farmer keeps sheep, cows, ducks, hens and chickens.

For dinner there was chicken, potatoes, peas and carrots.

Dad went to buy apples, cheese, rice and flour.

In the toy box I found marbles, bricks, paints and a teddy bear.

Put the plates, knives, forks and spoons on the table.

> Any items are acceptable as long as they fit the context and are correctly separated with commas.
>
> Check that no comma has been added before 'and'. The sentence should end with a full stop.

Sentence practice

Write a sentence with a list of <u>three</u> or more foods that you like. Check your **punctuation**.

I like ice cream, chocolate, pasta, fish fingers and apples.

25

> This is an example of an acceptable sentence. It must contain at least three items correctly separated with commas, and with no comma added before 'and'.

Lesson 19 Verbs with –ing: present tense

Focus introducing the progressive form of verbs in the present tense [used to show actions in progress]

Key terms verb, present tense

Focus text I am sitting by the door. I am waiting for my mum.
Amit is standing by the coat hooks. He is putting on his coat.
The twins are gazing out of the window. They are looking for
their dad.

TEACH

Show the focus text and read it aloud. Discuss the scene and the actions of the characters. Ask the children to identify the verbs – the words that describe what the characters are doing [e.g. standing; waiting]. Ask the children what they notice about these highlighted verbs [e.g. they all end with –ing; there is an extra verb before each of them – 'am'/'is'/'are'].

Discuss whether the text is in the past tense or present tense [present tense – the events are happening right now].

Explain that these sentences use a special form of verb for when actions progress or continue for a period of time. In the present tense, it shows that the events are happening – or are in progress – right now, as in the focus text. This is the progressive form. [Note: The children are not required to know the term 'progressive form' but you can introduce it if you wish.]

Use the focus text to look at how the progressive form of verbs is made up of two verbs: the –ing form of the verb and the 'helper' verb 'am'/'is'/'are' [e.g. am sitting; is standing]. Show that the sentences would not make sense without the helper verb [e.g. He putting on his coat.].

Explain that these extra helper verbs also tell us the tense – *when* the action takes place. In the present tense, we use am/is/are. Which helper verb we use depends on who the sentence is about, as in the focus text [I am, he is, they are]. [Note: This is covered in more detail in Lesson 27.]

EXTEND Explore how the helper verb changes depending whether the subject of the sentence is singular or plural.

PRACTISE

Pupil book page 26

APPLY

- The children write sentences to say 'what I am doing right now' [e.g. I am writing ...; I am hoping ...].
- The children write descriptions of the weather right now, using progressive forms [e.g. Raindrops are bouncing in puddles. The wind is swirling ... Empty crisp packets are blowing ...].
- Challenge the children to describe what is happening in a painting or picture using progressive verb forms [e.g. Two boys are ...; The lady is ...].
- The children act out events in a story and write a commentary [e.g. Cinderella is dancing. People are watching.].

ASSESS

Dictation: The sun shines and the children run on to the beach.
Say: Underline the verbs in this sentence. Now write the sentence using –ing verb forms.
Answer: The sun is shining and the children are running on to the beach.
Check: The –ing verbs are spelt correctly and the sentence is correctly punctuated.

Pupil book answers

Verbs with –ing: present tense

> **Remember**
>
> In the **present tense**, you use the **–ing verb** form with the 'helper' verbs '**am**', '**is**' or '**are**'. These verbs show that an action is carrying on for some time.
>
> I am waiting for my mum.
> Amit is putting on his coat.
> The twins are gazing out of the window.

Try it

1 Complete each sentence using the correct form of the **verb**.

They are _____digging_____ a hole.   (dig)

The boy is _____banging_____ the drum.   (bang)

We are _____learning_____ to play hockey.   (learn)

I am _____drinking_____ my milk.   (drink)

My sister is _____smiling_____ at me.   (smile)

2 Complete each sentence in the **present tense**, using the **–ing** form of a **verb**.

The ducks _____are swimming_____ on the pond.

The clock in the hall _____is ticking_____ .

The farmer _____is feeding_____ the hens.

Vikesh _____is going_____ for a walk.

I _____am waiting_____ for the bus.

Sentence practice

Write a sentence about what you are doing right now, using an **–ing verb** form.

I am thinking of a good sentence.

The verbs should be spelt correctly, including any that require a change to the spelling [e.g. smiling]. Revise these spelling patterns if necessary [e.g. dropping the final 'e' when adding –ing; doubling the final consonant when adding –ing].

Other verbs are acceptable as long as they make sense and use the –ing form. The verbs should be in the present tense and be spelt correctly, including those where a change is needed [e.g. swimming].

The children's answers may show difficulties with subject–verb agreement [the use of 'am'/'is'/'are']. Some children pick this up naturally; others find it difficult. It is covered in more detail in Lesson 27, but it is important to point out the correct choice so that the children become familiar with the correct patterns.

This is an example of an appropriate sentence using an –ing verb form. The –ing verb should be spelt correctly.

Check that the children have used 'I am', not 'I is'.

Lesson 20 Verbs with –ing: past tense

Focus introducing the progressive form of verbs in the past tense; changing tense

Key terms verb, tense, present tense, past tense

Focus text **It is raining. James is reading. Alfie is playing with his car. Katie and Beth are drawing pictures.**

TEACH

Show the focus text and read it aloud. Discuss the scene and the actions of the characters. Ask: What tense is this? [present tense – the events are happening right now] Recap the progressive [–ing] form of verbs in the present tense. Remind the children that this form of verb is used when the actions are still in progress and still happening right now.

Explain that you are going to change the focus text into the past tense, as if it were a story. Go through the text, reading each sentence aloud and changing 'is' to 'was' and 'are' to 'were'. Then read the new past tense version aloud to hear the effect.

Explain that the text still uses the progressive or –ing form of verbs but it is now in the past tense – as if the events were happening in the past, not happening now. Explain that this verb form is used to show that the events 'progressed' or *were* happening for some time [e.g. it was raining for some time; James was reading for some time].

Discuss how you changed the focus text from the present tense to the past tense, noting that it is the extra helper verb that you changed, not the verb ending with –ing. Point out that in the past tense we use 'was' instead of 'is' and 'were' instead of 'are'.

Explain that, as with the present tense, the helper verb depends on who or what the sentence is about [the subject] – so, for example, 'I/she/he was' or 'you/they/we were'. [Note: Again, this will be covered in more detail in Lesson 27.]

EXTEND Explore how the verb changes to match the subject [e.g. The boy was running. The boys <u>were</u> running.].

PRACTISE

Pupil book page 27

APPLY

- When reading stories, look for examples of sentences using past progressive verb forms, such as when actions in progress are interrupted [e.g. Cinderella was sweeping the floor when …]. Encourage the children to write their own sentences using these as models.
- Ask the children to use an –ing verb form when writing an account, to show that an event was happening for some time [e.g. Dad was feeding the ducks.]. Instruct the children to underline the verb.
- The children write the opening line of a story using an –ing verb form [e.g. One day Sasha was walking home from school …].
- Challenge the children to use progressive forms to write sentences saying what was happening five minutes, an hour or two hours ago [e.g. I was getting up. We were coming to school.].

ASSESS

Dictation: I am hiding in the shed and Sam is looking for me.
Say: This sentence is in the present tense. Write it in the past tense.
Answer: I was hiding in the shed and Sam was looking for me.
Check: The verbs are spelt correctly and the sentence is correctly punctuated.

Pupil book answers

Verbs with –ing: past tense

Remember

In the **past tense**, you use the **–ing verb** form with the 'helper' verbs 'was' or 'were'. These verbs show that an action was carrying on for some time.

It was raining. James was reading.
Katie and Beth were drawing pictures.

Try it

1 Decide if each sentence is in the **past tense** or the **present tense**. Write 'past tense' or 'present tense'.

He is going to the shops.   present tense

The stars were shining brightly.   past tense

The tap was dripping in the sink.   past tense

I am baking a cake for tea.   present tense

Omar and Jess are having lunch.   present tense

2 These sentences are in the present tense. Rewrite them in the **past tense**.

The man is pointing at me. The man was pointing at me.

The eagles are flying. The eagles were flying.

I am looking for you. I was looking for you.

The boys are playing. The boys were playing.

Dad is talking to us. Dad was talking to us.

> Check that the children use 'were' after 'The eagles ...' and 'The boys'. Plural agreement is covered again in Lesson 27.

Sentence practice

Write a sentence in the **past tense** to say what Red Riding Hood was doing in the woods.

Red Riding Hood was visiting her grandma.

27

> This is just an example of a possible sentence. The sentence should be in the past tense and use a progressive form.

Revision 2 answers

This page revises the children's understanding of the terms 'noun', 'verb' and 'adjective', which have now been introduced. It is important to encourage them to think about how the words function in a sentence when identifying word classes. The focus of each activity is given to help identify areas where the children need further reinforcement.

Focus: identifying nouns

Remind the children that nouns are words that name things. They are often preceded by 'the' or 'a'.

Focus: identifying adjectives

Remind the children that adjectives tell us more about nouns. They often appear directly before the noun.

Focus: identifying verbs

Remind the children that a verb can either be a 'doing word' or a 'being word' [e.g. is; was; have]. Another good way of identifying verbs is that they change tense [e.g. is/was; have/had].

Two words should be underlined in each sentence. Check that 'painting' is not underlined, as here it is a noun [*the* painting].

Revision 2

1 Underline the <u>three</u> **nouns** in each sentence.

A <u>clock</u> stood in the <u>corner</u> of the <u>room</u>.

A <u>giraffe</u> has a long <u>neck</u> that can reach the top <u>branches</u>.

The old <u>woman</u> was polishing the <u>windows</u> with a yellow <u>duster</u>.

The little <u>boy</u> went to fill the <u>bucket</u> at the <u>well</u>.

2 Underline the **adjective** in each sentence.

The <u>little</u> pony jumped over the fence and galloped off.

The <u>clever</u> rabbit tricked the crocodile.

The parrot stretched his <u>beautiful</u> wings.

Where did I put my <u>green</u> bag?

3 Underline the **verbs** in each sentence.

It <u>was</u> cold this morning so I <u>wore</u> my thickest socks.

I <u>have</u> a new game and I <u>play</u> it all the time.

The old man <u>smiled</u> when he <u>hung</u> the painting on the wall.

I <u>read</u> my book and then I <u>go</u> to bed.

4 Use **un–** to change the meaning of the underlined **adjective** in each sentence. Write the new adjective.

The race was <u>fair</u>.   unfair

Joel was the <u>lucky</u> little boy.   unlucky

The children were <u>friendly</u> at her new school.   unfriendly

Focus: identifying adjectives and using the prefix un– to change their meaning

Remind the children that the prefix un– changes the meaning of adjectives so that they mean the opposite.

This page revises the children's understanding of sentence and grammar concepts introduced in Section 1. The focus of each activity is given to help identify areas that need further reinforcement.

Schofield & Sims **Grammar and Punctuation**   Grammar 2

5 Write the missing **punctuation mark** to complete each sentence.

How amazing _!_

I am planning a party_._

How did he do it_?_

What a surprise_!_

She went for a run_._

Do you like peas_?_

6 Draw lines to match each sentence to the correct **sentence type**.

The thief is getting away.

Stop that man.

Leah has a meeting.

Meet me on the corner.

Don't run on the grass.

statement

command

7 There is a **punctuation mark** missing from this writing. Rewrite it correctly.

Class 3 went swimming Simon swam right across the pool.

Class 3 went swimming. Simon swam right across the pool.

8 These **verbs** are in the **present tense**. Rewrite them in the **past tense**.

We <u>mix</u> the pudding in the bowl.   mixed

I <u>bake</u> a pie and Mum <u>makes</u> a cake.   baked   made

Mum <u>passes</u> me a sandwich and I <u>eat</u> it.   passed   ate

29

Focus: sentence types – statements, questions, exclamations; end-of-sentence punctuation

The children need to identify the grammatical patterns of the sentences to choose the correct punctuation mark.

Focus: sentence types – statements and commands

The children need to identify the grammatical patterns of statements and commands [e.g. statements start with the subject of the sentence; commands begin with a verb].

Focus: demarcating sentence boundaries with full stops

The children need to identify the end of a sentence and correctly insert the full stop.

Focus: simple past and present tense; regular and familiar irregular verbs

The past tense verbs should be spelt correctly.

Writing task 2: Analysis sheet

Tick the circles to show amount of evidence found in writing:

1 No evidence
2 Some evidence
3 Clear evidence

Pupil name: _____

Date: _____

Assessing punctuation

The writing sample demonstrates:	Evidence		
capital letters used at the beginning of sentences.	①	②	③
sentence boundaries recognised and demarcated with full stops.	①	②	③
question marks and exclamation marks used when required.	①	②	③
capital letters used for 'I', names of people and places, and days of the week.	①	②	③
commas to separate items in a list [e.g. Parrots eat fruit, seeds and nuts.].	①	②	③

Assessing grammar and sentence structure

The writing sample demonstrates:	Evidence		
grammatically correct sentences.	①	②	③
different sentence types [e.g. statements about the animal].	①	②	③
co-ordinating conjunctions [and, but, or] to join words or clauses [e.g. They live in gardens and they eat worms ...; Some dogs ... but my dog ...].	①	②	③
subordinating conjunctions [because, when, if, that] to add more detail [e.g. Dogs bark when/if ...; I like pandas because ...].	①	②	③
correct use of tense [present tense to describe and give information].	①	②	③
appropriate use of adjectives to describe the animal [e.g. It has floppy ears ...; They have long tails ...; A lion is bigger than ...].	①	②	③
expanded noun phrases to specify [e.g. the male lion].	①	②	③

Key target: _____

*From: **Grammar 2 Teacher's Guide** © Schofield & Sims Ltd, 2017. This page may be photocopied after purchase.*

Writing task 2: Pupil checklist

Name: _____   Date: _____

Reread what you have written to check that it makes sense. Tick the circle if you have correctly used the punctuation or grammar feature in your writing.

Punctuation

◯ I have used capital letters at the beginning of sentences.

◯ I have used full stops at the end of sentences.

◯ I have used a question mark or exclamation mark if it is needed.

◯ I have used capital letters for 'I', names of people and places, and days of the week.

◯ I have used commas to separate items in a list.

Grammar and sentences

◯ I have written in sentences and they make sense.

◯ I have used different sentence types (for example, statements).

◯ I have used 'and', 'but', 'or' to make some longer sentences.

◯ I have used 'because', 'when', 'that', 'if' to add more information to a sentence.

◯ I have used present tense verbs to describe and give information.

◯ I have used some adjectives to describe the animal (for example, floppy ears).

◯ I have used nouns and noun phrases (for example, the male lion).

Teacher feedback

My key target: _____

_____

From: **Grammar 2 Teacher's Guide** © *Schofield & Sims Ltd, 2017. This page may be photocopied after purchase.*

Lesson 21   Adverbs

Focus   introducing adverbs; identifying and using 'how' adverbs in a sentence

Key terms   **adverb**, verb, adjective, noun

Focus text   She crept quietly into the kitchen. She carefully lifted the key from the hook and opened the back door slowly. She called softly into the moonlight.

TEACH

Show the focus text and read it aloud. Invite a child to act out the actions described. Discuss the events and the character's actions [e.g. What time of day is it? What might she be doing?].

Read each sentence and discuss the purpose of the highlighted words. Establish that these words describe how each action was performed. Read the text without the adverbs. Ask: Why are these words used? [e.g. they add more detail; they add mystery; they make the character's actions sound secretive]

Explain that the highlighted words are called adverbs: they tell us *how* the action in a sentence is performed, by adding more detail to the verb. Compare this to adjectives: they add more detail, or tell us more, about a noun.

[Note: Adverbs can also give detail about *where* or *when* the action is performed, and they can be used with adjectives as well as verbs. However, these other uses of adverbs are covered later in the programme, so there is no need to introduce this material at this point.]

Use the focus text to look at where the adverbs are placed in relation to the verb or action [e.g. crept quietly; called softly; opened the door slowly]. Invite the children to suggest other 'how' adverbs to use in these phrases [e.g. crept silently; called loudly; opened the door quickly].

The children may notice that all the adverbs in the focus text end –ly, and this is true of many 'how' adverbs. [Note: Forming adverbs using the suffix –ly is the focus of the next lesson, Lesson 22.] However, you may wish to explain that not all adverbs end with –ly [e.g. 'she stood still' – where 'still' is an adverb, telling us more about how she stood].

EXTEND   Discuss other examples of 'how' adverbs that do not end with –ly [e.g. She ran fast.].

PRACTISE

Pupil book page 32

APPLY

- When reading stories, ask the children to identify examples of adverbs. Discuss why they are used.
- When revising stories they have written, encourage the children to look for an opportunity to add an adverb to say *how* a character performed an action.
- Encourage the use of simple adverbs in instructions to say how a task should be done [e.g. Slice the bread carefully].
- The children write list poems using an adverb in every line [e.g. silently – 'Cats prowl silently, Snow falls silently'; slowly – 'Snails crawl slowly, Weeks pass slowly'].

ASSESS

Dictation: The fox ran <u>swiftly</u> across the snowy field.
Say: Underline the adverb in the sentence.

Pupil book answers

Adverbs

Remember

An **adverb** is a word that tells you more about how an action is carried out.

She <u>opened</u> the back door slowly.
She <u>called</u> softly into the moonlight.

Try it

1 Underline the **adverb** in each sentence.

The door slid <u>silently</u> open.

She rocked the baby <u>gently</u> as she sang.

I placed the book <u>carefully</u> on the shelf.

We sat <u>happily</u> and watched the rabbits play.

The cat purred and swished her tail <u>lazily</u>.

2 Rewrite each sentence, adding a suitable **adverb**.

Flags flap in the wind. Flags flap wildly in the wind.

The firework went off. The firework went off suddenly.

Dad turned off the leaky tap. Dad quickly turned off the leaky tap.

The sick child moaned. The sick child moaned loudly.

Tom made his way home. Tom made his way slowly home.

These are examples of suitable adverbs. The children may choose different adverbs or use them in different positions in the sentence. Discuss these variations.

Sentence practice

Write a sentence using the **adverb** 'quietly'.

The children sat quietly and listened to the teacher.

32

This is an example of a possible sentence. It should include an appropriate use of the adverb 'quietly'.
Check that the sentence is correctly punctuated.

Lesson 22 Adverbs with suffix –ly

Focus forming adverbs by adding the suffix –ly to adjectives

Key terms adjective, adverb, suffix

Focus text Mr Hodges was kind.
He spoke kindly to everyone.

TEACH

Show the first sentence of the focus text. Discuss what type of word is highlighted [an adjective – it describes the person, Mr Hodges].

Show the second sentence. Discuss what type of word is highlighted in this sentence [an adverb – it tells us more about the verb, or *how* Mr Hodges spoke].

Explain that many adverbs that describe *how* actions are performed are formed by adding the suffix –ly to an adjective. The word 'kind' is an adjective as it describes the man; 'kindly' is an adverb because it describes his actions.

Use a different adjective in the first sentence of the focus text [e.g. Mr Hodges was sad.]. Invite the children to provide the adverb to complete the second sentence [e.g. He spoke sadly.]. Repeat with other adjectives [e.g. mean; calm; fair], writing the corresponding adverbs on the board so the children can see the suffix –ly added to the adjective [e.g. meanly; calmly; fairly].

You may wish to point out that not all words ending with –ly are adverbs [e.g. a friendly boy; a lovely idea; a woolly jumper]. These words describe or tell us more about a noun rather than a verb, so they are adjectives. They are also formed from nouns [friend, love, wool] rather than adjectives.

EXTEND Look at adding –ly to words already ending with a suffix [e.g. carefully; carelessly; foolishly].

PRACTISE

Pupil book page 33

APPLY

- Collect lists of adverbs ending with –ly and display them. Encourage the children to use these words in their writing.
- Encourage the children to use adverbs ending with –ly when writing about the actions of characters in stories [e.g. sadly; quietly].
- Draw attention to the use of adverbs ending with –ly in other subjects [e.g. in PE, describing how to perform movements – 'gently'; 'smoothly'; in music, describing how to sing or play – 'loudly'; 'quietly'; 'quickly'; 'brightly'; 'slowly'].
- The children write a list poem using a different adverb ending with –ly in each line [e.g. a poem about mini-beasts: 'Snails creep slowly, Spiders scuttle speedily'].

ASSESS

Dictation: Sit down. Write your name <u>neatly</u> at the top of the page.
Say: Underline the adverb ending with the suffix –ly. Now add another adverb ending with –ly to the first sentence.
Answer: e.g. Sit down quietly.
Check: Both sentences are correctly punctuated. Adverbs ending with –ly should be spelt correctly.

Pupil book answers

Adverbs with suffix –ly

Remember

You can make lots of **adverbs** by adding the **suffix –ly** to an **adjective**.

Mr Hodges was kind.   (adjective)
He spoke kind<u>ly</u>.   (adverb)

Try it

1 Add the **suffix –ly** to each **adjective** to make it into an **adverb**. Write the adverb.

brave	bravely	sweet	sweetly
proud	proudly	smooth	smoothly
smart	smartly	bad	badly
sad	sadly	selfish	selfishly
secret	secretly	safe	safely

> The adverbs should be spelt correctly. Check the words ending with 'e' [bravely, safely]. Adding the suffix –ly to these words requires no change in spelling.

2 Choose the best **adverb** from the activity above to complete each sentence.

The lifeguard dived ___bravely___ into the water.

Grandpa dressed ___smartly___ in his best suit.

The plane landed ___smoothly___ on the runway.

The team played ___badly___ in the second half.

She wore the medal ___proudly___ for the rest of the day.

> The children need to understand the meaning of the adverbs in the first activity to use them in the correct context. Accept other answers if the choice clearly fits the context of the sentence. The adverbs should be spelt correctly.

Sentence practice

Make the **adjective** 'fierce' into an **adverb**. Use the adverb to write a sentence.

The lion roared fiercely at the other animals.

33

> This is an example of a suitable sentence. Do not accept sentences that use the adjective 'fierce' rather than the adverb 'fiercely'. The adverb should be spelt correctly – again, no change in spelling is required when adding –ly to this adjective.

Lesson 23 Apostrophes in shortened forms

Focus using apostrophes to mark where letters are missing in contracted forms

Key terms **apostrophe**, punctuation mark

Focus text **Alex:** (*feeling his way*) I am coming but it is dark in here.
I cannot see the way. Ouch! Now I have stubbed my toe.
Do not laugh at me.

TEACH

Show the focus text and read it aloud. Invite the children to act out the events and speak the words of the character, Alex, as they are written. Discuss why this sounds strange. Ask: Do we normally speak like this? Would we say 'I am coming'? [no – we would probably say 'I'm coming']

Explain that you are going to make it sound more like normal speech by changing some of the words. Read the first sentence and change the highlighted words to 'I'm' and 'it's'. Write the shortened form directly above the existing words so it is easy to compare them. Ask the children if they can supply the shortened forms for the remaining sentences [can't, I've, Don't]. Again, write these words above the originals. Read the completed version aloud to show that it now sounds more like normal speech.

Explain that we often use these shortened forms in speech and sometimes in writing. The two words are pushed together to become one word. [Note: This is sometimes called a contraction – the words are contracted together. The children are not yet required to know the term 'contraction', but you can introduce it if you wish.] Explain that a punctuation mark called an apostrophe is used in these shortened forms in place of the missing letters.

Use the changes you made to the focus text to show how the apostrophe is used. Point out that when the two words are pushed [contracted] into one, there are always some letters missing. The apostrophe goes where the missing letters would be. You can demonstrate this with the pupils holding up letter cards if you wish. The word 'don't' is a particularly useful example to show that the apostrophe goes in place of the missing letters, rather than at the point where the words join together.

EXTEND Explore further contractions, including some that feature confusing homophones [e.g. 'they're' and 'there'/'their'].

PRACTISE

Pupil book page 34

APPLY

- The children write speech bubbles for characters in stories that include a shortened form [e.g. Who's been sleeping in my bed?].
- The children write a postcard including shortened forms [e.g. I'm on holiday in Devon. I've been swimming. I'll see you soon.].
- Working in partners, the children act out a short scene between two friends and then write it as a play script using shortened forms.
- Together, look for shortened forms when reading dialogue in stories and decide on the full form of the word [e.g. Who's there?/Who is there?].

ASSESS

Dictation: It isn't fair. You've had a turn and I haven't.
Say: Check your punctuation.
Check: The contracted forms have the correct spelling and placement of the apostrophe.

Pupil book answers

Apostrophes in shortened forms

Remember

Sometimes two words are pushed together to make one word. Some letters are missed out. You write an **apostrophe** in place of the missing letters.

I am coming. ⟶ I'm coming.
Do not laugh. ⟶ Don't laugh.

Try it

1 Rewrite each underlined shortened word with the **apostrophe** in the correct place.

I have	Ive	I've	she is	shes	she's
was not	wasnt	wasn't	they will	theyll	they'll
I would	Id	I'd	we are	were	we're
cannot	cant	can't	he would	hed	he'd

2 Write the underlined words as <u>one</u> word, using an **apostrophe**.

It <u>has not</u> been raining for long. ___hasn't___

<u>I will</u> be home soon. ___I'll___

I think <u>it is</u> a great idea. ___it's___

<u>It has</u> been a long time. ___It's___

I <u>could not</u> help it. ___couldn't___

Sentence practice

Write the words 'did not' as <u>one</u> word with an **apostrophe**. Use the word in a sentence.

We didn't stop for lunch.

34

Check for correct spelling and correct placement of the apostrophe. The pronoun 'I' in the first and third sentences must be written with a capital letter.

Again, check for correct spelling and correct placement of the apostrophe. The pronoun 'I' must be written with a capital letter in the second example. The contraction in the fourth example should also begin with a capital letter as it is at the start of a sentence.

You may wish to discuss how 'it's' can mean both 'it is' and 'it has'.

Correct spelling and correct placement of the apostrophe are required. Any sentence using 'didn't' is acceptable.

Lesson 24 Apostrophes for possession

Focus using apostrophes to mark possession in singular nouns

Key terms apostrophe, punctuation mark

Focus text Cinderella   bowl of porridge
            Baby Bear   sack of gold
            the giant   glass slipper

TEACH

Show the focus text. Invite the children to match the possessions to the story characters [e.g. Ask: Who does the glass slipper belong to?]. For each answer draw a line to match the character and the possession and say the possessive phrase [e.g. Cinderella's glass slipper]. In colour, add 'apostrophe s' after the name of the character. Ask the children to name the punctuation mark you have added [an apostrophe].

Invite the children to suggest some more examples of characters and their possessions to add to the list in the focus text [e.g. Grandma's nightcap; the troll's bridge]. Add the suggestions, again writing the 'apostrophe s' in colour.

Explain that the apostrophe is a punctuation mark with two different uses. An apostrophe is used in shortened forms of words but it is also used with the letter 's' to show possession – that something belongs to someone or something.

Pick up some items around the classroom and ask: Whose is this? Invite the children to respond by naming the owner [e.g. Amy's]. Write labels to attach to the possessions [e.g. Amy's pencil case], making it clear that you are adding 'apostrophe s' after the person's name.

EXTEND Find examples of apostrophes in books or in the classroom. Discuss whether they are apostrophes used in shortened forms or apostrophes to show possession.

PRACTISE

Pupil book page 35

APPLY

- The children use 'apostrophe s' with characters' names when writing a traditional story [e.g. Red Riding Hood – Granny's cottage/bed/hands/eyes/teeth; Goldilocks – Baby Bear's bowl/chair/bed].
- Encourage the use of 'apostrophe s' when writing personal accounts of events [e.g. Dad's car; Mum's birthday].
- Write labels for classroom displays of objects or photographs using an apostrophe for possession [e.g. Jessie's model of a spaceship].
- The children write descriptions of people or animals using possessive apostrophes to describe features [e.g. Jack's hair is brown. Emily's eyes are green. An elephant's trunk is long.].
- Challenge the children to write a story with patterned language that uses a possessive apostrophe [e.g. He tried the bird's nest but it was too twiggy. He tried the rabbit's burrow but it was too dark.].

ASSESS

Dictation: I haven't seen the <u>king's</u> golden slippers.
Say: Underline the word that has an apostrophe to show that something belongs to someone.
Check: Both 'haven't' and 'king's' have the correct spelling and placement of the apostrophe.

Pupil book answers

Apostrophes for possession

Remember

You use an **apostrophe** with **–s** to show that something belongs to someone or something.

Cinderella's glass slipper   the giant's sack of gold

Try it

1 Underline the word that has an **apostrophe** to show that something belongs to someone or something.

I haven't seen <u>Daniel's</u> book.

Don't eat <u>Baby Bear's</u> porridge.

<u>Holly's</u> jumper isn't here.

I didn't hear the <u>teacher's</u> whistle.

I can't find the <u>cat's</u> collar.

You could discuss the contractions in these sentences [e.g. which word is shortened and which letter is missing].

2 Rewrite the sentence, adding an **apostrophe** with **–s** to show that something belongs to someone or something.

Cinderella sisters were mean. Cinderella's sisters were mean.

This is Jason bag. This is Jason's bag.

Is this Mum plate? Is this Mum's plate?

Tara hair is black. Tara's hair is black.

I found my sister pen. I found my sister's pen.

Sentence practice

Write a sentence to describe a hat belonging to a wizard, using an **apostrophe**.

The wizard's hat was tall and pointy.

35

This is an example of a possible sentence. It must contain the phrase 'wizard's hat', with the apostrophe in the correct position.

Lesson 25 Nouns with suffixes –er, –ness, –ment

Focus forming nouns using the suffixes –ness, –ment, –er

Key terms noun, suffix, verb, adjective

Focus text **The painter read the statement from the king and his heart was filled with sadness.**

TEACH

Show the focus text. Ask: Did the king's statement contain good news? What makes you say that? [the painter's reaction – he was 'filled with sadness']

Ask the children to identify the five nouns in the sentence [painter, statement, king, heart, sadness]. Underline the words as they are identified. The word 'sadness' is not an obvious noun – it does not name a person or a physical thing [and here it is not preceded by 'the'/'a']. Show the children that it is a noun by using it with 'the' [e.g. the sadness in his heart].

Explain that three of the nouns in the sentence are formed by adding a suffix to a word. Ask if the children can spot them [painter, statement, sadness]. Use a different colour to write over the suffixes.

Explain that suffixes such as –er, –ness and –ment are added to words to form nouns. Use the focus text to discuss how they are used and what sorts of nouns are formed.

The suffix –er takes a verb [e.g. paint] and makes it into a noun that names a person or thing that does that action [a painter]. Ask the children to suggest other nouns ending with –er to use in place of 'painter' in the focus text [e.g. farmer; teacher; driver].

The suffix –ness takes an adjective [e.g. sad] and makes it into a noun that names the state of that feeling [e.g. sadness – the state of feeling sad]. Nouns like this do not name physical objects but states of feeling or sensing [e.g. sadness; illness]. [Note: They are sometimes called abstract nouns but the children do not yet need to know this term.]

The suffix –ment takes a verb [e.g. state] and makes it into a noun [statement].

EXTEND Explore nouns formed using other suffixes [e.g. freedom; championship].

PRACTISE

Pupil book page 36

APPLY

- The children use nouns ending with –er to write names for 'Happy Families' characters [e.g. Mr Bun the baker; Miss Spade the gardener].
- The children write descriptive sentences, or lines for a list poem, about a state of feeling [e.g. Sadness is ...; Happiness is ...; Kindness is ...].
- Look for opportunities to use nouns with these suffixes in other subjects [e.g. testing qualities of materials in science – bendiness; stiffness; smoothness; softness; designing useful items in design and technology – a buzzer; a slider; a drink holder].

ASSESS

Dictation: The hunter hid in the darkness of the cave. She waited for a movement.
Say: Underline the three nouns with suffixes.
Check: The nouns are all spelt correctly and both sentences are correctly punctuated.

Pupil book answers

Nouns with suffixes –er, –ness, –ment

Remember

Some **nouns** are made by adding a **suffix** to the end of another word.

painter   sadness   statement

Try it

1 Add the correct **suffix**, **–er**, **–ness** or **–ment**, to make each word into a **noun**.

enjoy _ment_   teach _er_

sick _ness_   play _er_

work _er_   fair _ness_

amaze _ment_   punish _ment_

shy _ness_   amuse _ment_

Do not accept answers that are comparative adjectives rather than nouns [e.g. fairer].

The noun should be spelt correctly. No change in spelling is required when adding the suffixes to these words.

2 Add the correct **suffix** to complete the word in **bold**.

Jogging helped Sarah improve her **fit** _ness_ .

The **garden** _er_ cut the grass.

I was dazzled by the **bright** _ness_ of the sunlight.

He went to hospital for **treat** _ment_ .

Dad wrote a **remind** _er_ about the milk.

Sentence practice

Add a **suffix** to make the word 'kind' into a **noun**. Write a sentence using the noun you have made.

Gran thanked me for my kindness.

36

This is an example of a suitable sentence using the word 'kindness' in context.

Lesson 26 Proper nouns

Focus introducing the term 'proper noun'; revising capital letters for names

Key terms noun, **proper noun**, capital letter

Focus text I met a boy and his brother outside the school.
I met Adam Smith and his brother Jamie outside Hill Street School.

TEACH

Show the focus text. Read the first sentence and discuss what type of word is highlighted [nouns]. Read the second sentence and compare the two sentences. Discuss how they are different, which sentence is better and why [e.g. the second sentence is more specific about who and where; the people and places have real names].

Explain that names, like those in the second sentence, are a special type of noun called proper nouns. Ordinary or common nouns, like those in the first sentence, just refer generally to a boy, a brother, a school. Proper nouns are the names given to specific people, places or things. It is a proper noun because it has a 'proper' name, or a name of its own.

Remind the children that names, or proper nouns, always start with a capital letter. Look at the focus text and count how many capital letters are used in each sentence. Ask: Why are there more capital letters in the second sentence? [e.g. the three proper nouns all need capital letters; the ordinary nouns do not need capitals] Point out that in 'Hill Street School' all the words in the name need a capital letter.

Say some common nouns and invite the children to suggest a suitable proper noun naming a particular person or place [e.g. a school – Greet Primary School; a man – Mr Hills; Wayne Rooney; Superman]. Ask the children to orally compose a sentence using some of these proper nouns. Encourage them to make it as interesting as possible [e.g. I met Mr Hills and his dog Oscar outside Green Lane Primary School.]. Write the sentence, discussing when to use a capital letter.

EXTEND Look at how capital letters are used in titles, headings and poems.

PRACTISE

Pupil book page 37

APPLY

- Identify proper nouns in history [e.g. people's names; places] or geography [e.g. countries; oceans; capital cities]. Remind the children to use capital letters for these words when writing.
- The children write directions around the local area using street names and the names of local landmarks.
- Encourage the children to make up interesting names for characters and places in stories.
- In accounts of events, encourage the use of proper nouns rather than common nouns [e.g. 'We went to Chester Zoo.' rather than 'We went to the zoo.'].
- In all of the above, the children proofread writing to check that capital letters have been used for proper nouns.

ASSESS

Dictation: Mr Andrews visited Blackpool Tower on his way to Scotland.
Say: Underline the proper nouns.
Check: All the proper nouns begin with capital letters.

Pupil book answers

Proper nouns

Remember

A **proper noun** is a special noun that you use to name a person, place or thing. A proper noun always starts with a **capital letter**.

I met Adam Smith and his brother Jamie outside Hill Street School.

Try it

1 Underline all the **proper nouns** in these sentences. Give them a **capital letter**.

I think harry is in mr jackson's class at marshmead school.
H   M J   M S

We watched a film of neil armstrong taking off in apollo 11.
N A   A

Once upon a time, king marcus lived in rockington palace.
K   M   R   P

We went to chester zoo with mr davies.
C   Z   M D

Mum said mrs patel moved to grove road in june.
M P   G   R   J

2 Rewrite each sentence, using **proper nouns** in place of the underlined noun phrases. Remember to use **capital letters**.

A man went to town. Mr Higgins went to Hanbury.

The teacher helped the boy. Mrs Patel helped Bobby Brown.

The girl lived in a cottage. Ruby lived in Rose Cottage.

The boy goes to school. Josh goes to Stockwell Primary School.

These are just examples of suitable sentences. Compare the children's choices. Capital letters must be used for the proper nouns. The sentences should also be punctuated correctly.

Sentence practice

Write a sentence with two **proper nouns** in it.

Samantha Robinson goes to Newtown Road School.

37

This is an example of a suitable sentence. Capital letters must be used for the proper nouns. The sentence should be punctuated correctly.

Lesson 27 **Plural nouns and verbs**

Focus using the correct verbs to match singular and plural nouns

Key terms verb, noun, singular, plural, suffix

Focus text The autumn sky is grey.
The bird has flown away.
The morning feels cold.
The tree is turning gold.

TEACH

Show the focus text and read it aloud. Discuss the subject of the poem and what is described in each line. Underline the noun in each line [sky, bird, morning, tree]. Ask the children if these are singular or plural nouns [singular – there are no –s/–es endings].

Ask the children to help you change the nouns into plurals by adding –s/–es. As you do this, discuss the change in spelling needed for the word 'skies' [the 'y' changes to 'i' and –es is added, rather than –s].

Now read each line with the new plural noun and discuss how the verb needs to change to make it sound right [The skies are …, The birds have …, The mornings feel …, The trees are …].

Explain that a verb must match the noun that comes before it – a singular noun [one thing or person] needs a singular verb; a plural noun [more than one] needs a plural verb.

Use the focus text to look at examples of how different verbs change – so, for example, 'is' with singular nouns changes to 'are' with plural nouns; 'has' with singular nouns changes to 'have' with plural nouns; 'feels' with singular nouns changes to 'feel' with plural nouns.

Explain that it can be helpful to say sentences aloud to check that the verbs are correct [e.g. 'The trees *is* turning gold.' does not sound right]. Incorrect subject–verb agreement can be a problem in both speech and writing. [Note: This subject is covered again in **Grammar 3** but it is helpful if the children become aware of the correct patterns early on.]

EXTEND   Change the poem into the past tense using singular and then plural nouns.

PRACTISE

Pupil book page 38

APPLY

- The children write more lines for the poem 'Autumn' using both singular and plural forms [e.g. The berry turns red. The berries / Berries turn red.].
- The children write statements about a topic [e.g. types of transport] using singular and plural nouns [e.g. A car goes … Cars go …; A bus has … Buses have …].
- Encourage oral rehearsal of sentences before writing, and rereading after writing, to check that verbs have been used correctly.

ASSESS

Dictation: The fly buzzes round the jam pot.
Say: Write the sentence again, making the nouns in this sentence into plurals. Remember to change the verb as well.
Answer: The flies buzz round the jam pots.
Check: The plural nouns and the verbs are spelt correctly.

Pupil book answers

Plural nouns and verbs

Remember

A **noun** can be **singular** (just one) or **plural** (more than one). You need to use the correct **verb** to follow a singular or plural noun.

The bird has flown away. The birds have flown away.
The morning feels cold. The mornings feel cold.
The tree is turning gold. The trees are turning gold.

Try it

1 Choose the correct **verb** to follow each **plural noun**.

The boys ___shout___ as they run into the playground.   (shout shouts)

Two buses ___are___ coming down the road.   (is are)

Bulls ___have___ sharp horns.   (has have)

The toys ___go___ in the box.   (go goes)

The flowers ___grow___ in the garden.   (grow grows)

2 Rewrite each sentence, making the underlined **noun** a **plural**. Use the correct **verb**.

The hen is clucking. _The hens are clucking._

The fox sleeps in a den. _The foxes sleep in a den._

The house is very old. _The houses are very old._

The baby has blue eyes. _The babies have blue eyes._

The clown was funny. _The clowns were funny._

Both the plural nouns and the verbs should be spelt correctly.

Check that sentences begin with capital letters and end with full stops.

Sentence practice

Write a sentence using the **verbs** 'run' and 'runs'.

The cat runs off and the girls run after it.

38

This is an example of a suitable sentence using 'runs' with a singular noun and 'run' with a plural noun. Any plural noun is acceptable. It does not have to end with the suffixes –s or –es [e.g. The children run after it.].

The sentence should also begin with a capital letter and end with a full stop.

Lesson 28 Checking tense

Focus checking the consistent use of present or past tense throughout a piece of writing

Key terms verb, tense, past tense, present tense

Focus text Leo went to the park last Saturday. He met his friends and they play football all afternoon.

TEACH

Show the focus text. Read the first sentence and ask the children to say whether it is in the past tense or the present tense [past tense – the events happened last Saturday].

Read the second sentence. Ask the children if they notice anything wrong with this sentence [the verb 'play' is in the present tense]. Discuss what the correct word should be and write it in ['played' – the past tense of 'play'].

Explain that in a piece of writing we usually keep to the same tense – either past tense or present tense. An account of an event or a story, such as the focus text, is usually in the past tense. A factual report is usually in the present tense. The tense should not change unless there is a reason, such as at the end of an account where we might want to bring it up to date [e.g. I have the photos if you want to see them.].

Explain that an easy mistake is to start writing in the past tense and then switch to the present tense. Tell the children that when they read through their writing, they should check for changes in tense.

Use the focus text to remind the children that it is verbs that show the tense. Many past tense verbs are formed by adding –ed but sometimes a different word is needed [e.g. 'went' is the past tense of 'go'].

Invite the children to compose a further sentence for the focus text, maintaining the past tense. You could ask them to include a progressive form and/or to use a joining word or conjunction [e.g. They were looking for the ball when they saw a purse by the bench.].

EXTEND The children correct their own writing, checking that tense is used consistently.

PRACTISE

Pupil book page 39

APPLY

- The children write a story based on the focus text, maintaining the use of the past tense.
- When planning stories or accounts of events, remind the children to write down ideas or verbs in the past tense.
- When writing stories or accounts, remind the children to orally rehearse and to keep reading their writing to check that it stays in the past tense.
- After writing, the children work with a writing partner to read accounts or stories aloud and check that the past tense has been used consistently.
- Remind the children to maintain the use of the present tense when writing factual reports, explanations and definitions.

ASSESS

Dictation: Dean watched from the window and <u>sees</u> a spaceship landing.
Say: Underline the word that is wrong. Write it correctly.
Answer: saw
Check: The verbs are spelt correctly and the compound noun 'spaceship' is written as one word.

Pupil book answers

Checking tense

Remember

When you write, you usually keep to the same **tense** all through a piece of writing. Always check that the **verbs** show the correct tense.

Leo met his friends and they play played football all afternoon.

Try it

1 Underline the **verbs** in each sentence. Tick the box if the sentence keeps to the same **tense**.

Jake <u>jumped</u> off the swing and <u>ran</u> to the slide. ✓

Ladybirds <u>eat</u> greenfly and <u>lived</u> for about two years. ☐

Anya <u>sat</u> by the river and she <u>sees</u> a beautiful swan. ☐

He <u>walked</u> along the road and <u>heard</u> a crash. ✓

Noah <u>scrubbed</u> the washing and <u>hangs</u> it on the line. ☐

2 Complete each sentence using a **verb** in the correct **tense**.

Elijah saw his friends and he ___waved___ .

I was late but they ___waited___ for me.

The farmer gets up early and he ___milks___ the cows.

Andrew rolled over and he ___went___ back to sleep.

Spring is coming and the bears ___wake___ up.

Other verbs can fit into these sentences but they must be in the same tense as the first verb.

The verbs should be spelt correctly.

Sentence practice

Write a sentence to follow this one. Keep to the same **tense**.

Sophie looked up when she heard the car. She rushed to the door and flung it open.

39

This is an example of a suitable sentence that maintains the past tense of the given sentence. The sentence should be punctuated correctly.

Lesson 29 Longer noun phrases

> Focus   using expanded noun phrases to specify; expanding before and after the noun
>
> Key terms   noun, adjective, noun phrase
>
> Focus text   Which jumper would you like?
> the green jumper
> the large, blue jumper
> the red jumper with the stars

TEACH

Show the focus text and read it aloud. Ask the children to identify the noun and the adjectives in the first two noun phrases [jumper; green, large, blue]. Discuss why the adjectives are needed [e.g. they describe the jumper; they say which jumper is being referred to; they say which colour or size]. Discuss why two adjectives are needed in the second example [e.g. there might be two blue jumpers].

Look at the third noun phrase. Ask: This time, as well as an adjective, what else has been added? [an extra detail after the noun to say *which* red jumper]

Explain that these are all examples of noun phrases. A noun phrase is made up of a noun and any other words that go with the noun – this includes words like 'the'/'a' and words that add more detail about the noun, such as adjectives. We use longer noun phrases like these to describe things or to show clearly *which* noun we are talking about, as in the focus text.

Use the focus text to look at how words and extra phrases can be added to the noun to describe or specify. The first two noun phrases show how one or two adjectives can be added *before* the noun. The third noun phrase shows how a descriptive detail can also be added *after* the noun.

Invite the children to orally compose additional longer noun phrases to describe or specify a particular jumper [e.g. the pink, fluffy jumper with white spots].

EXTEND   Compose even longer noun phrases [e.g. the thick, purple jumper with green stripy sleeves].

PRACTISE

Pupil book page 40

APPLY

- The children write longer noun phrases to distinguish between similar items [e.g. fish in an aquarium; flowers in a garden – 'tall blue flowers on long stems', 'bright yellow flowers with red centres'].
- The children write longer noun phrases to use as clues to describe characters from stories [e.g. Goldilocks – 'the naughty little girl with golden hair'].
- When writing stories or accounts, ask the children to look for an opportunity to add a detail after a noun as well as using adjectives [e.g. an old lamp with a rusty handle].

ASSESS

Dictation: Greg was a <u>happy</u> <u>little</u> boy.
Say: Underline the adjectives in the noun phrase. Now add an extra detail *after* the noun.
Answer: e.g. Greg was a happy little boy with a big smile.

Pupil book answers

Longer noun phrases

> **Remember**
>
> In longer **noun phrases**, you add words to the **noun** to give more detail about it. You can add **adjectives** before the noun or other details after the noun.
>
> the green jumper
> the large, blue jumper
> the red jumper with the stars

Try it

1. Complete these **noun phrases**.

   the ___small___ ___wooden___ box on the shelf

   the ___beautiful___ ___green___ butterfly

   the little house with the bright red door

   the orange flowers in the silver vase

   the smart red car with a black stripe

These are only suggestions. Look for appropriate choices of adjective before the noun and phrases that add specifying detail after the noun. [Note: The children are not required to use commas to separate adjectives in their writing.]

Compare the children's answers to see the range of words chosen, and discuss interesting choices.

2. Write four **noun phrases** to describe different dogs. One has been done for you.

   the little fluffy dog in the basket

   the big scruffy dog in the kennel

   the spotty dog with long floppy ears

   the friendly dog with a happy bark

   the sleek black dog with a long thin tail

These are just suggestions. Look for phrases with one or two adjectives before the noun and an additional detail after the noun.

Discuss the children's choices. Which are the best noun phrases?

Sentence practice

Write a sentence about Annie's coat, using a longer **noun phrase**.

Annie has a dark green coat with a furry hood.

40

This is just a suggestion. Look for a noun phrase with one or two adjectives before the noun and an additional detail after the noun.

Lesson 30 Writing with joining words

> Focus using subordinating and co-ordinating conjunctions to improve a piece of writing
>
> Key terms sentence, joining word
>
> Focus text My dog is called Archie. He is a collie dog. He likes to run around outside. He does not like having a bath. I take Archie for a walk every day. He needs lots of exercise.

TEACH

Show the focus text and read it aloud. Invite the children to comment on what is good about it and what could be improved [e.g. all the sentences are quite short; there are no joining words].

Work together to improve the focus text by using joining words. Ask the children to suggest a joining word [conjunction] to join each pair of sentences [e.g. 'and' for the first two sentences; 'but' for the next two; 'because' for the last two].

Each time, model saying the new sentence, making the necessary changes including punctuation adjustments, and then rereading the new sentence. Once complete, read the new version of the text to hear the effect.

Explain that using joining words helps to improve our writing. Words such as 'and' and 'but' make our writing flow; words such as 'because' help expand ideas or join them together.

Use the changes to the focus text to recap how different joining words are used to join ideas in sentences [e.g. 'and' joins two equal ideas; 'but' joins two equal but contrasting ideas; 'because' gives a reason]. Ask the children if they can remember other joining words similar to 'because' that add extra information [e.g. 'when'; 'if'; 'that']. Invite the children to orally compose another sentence to add to the focus text using a different joining word [e.g. We take Archie to the vet if/when ...].

EXTEND Discuss alternative subordinating conjunctions for those used [e.g. 'as' in place of 'because' – 'I take Archie for a walk every day as he needs lots of exercise.'].

PRACTISE

Pupil book page 41

APPLY

- The children review a piece of their own writing to identify where a conjunction could be used to join two sentences. They then make the change, remembering to change the sentence punctuation.
- Make using joining words a target for all writing across the curriculum. Secure the use of 'and' and 'but', and begin to use 'when', 'because', 'that', 'if' or other joining words.
- Ask the children to highlight the joining words they use in a piece of writing.
- When writing stories, encourage the children to focus on using joining words to help sequence or connect events [e.g. The girl yelled when ...] and to develop character [e.g. He was frightened because ...].

ASSESS

Dictation: We went on the plane <u>and</u> we found our seats. I was scared <u>when</u> the plane took off.
Say: Underline the joining word in each sentence. Write another sentence to follow them, using a different joining word.
Answer: e.g. We had some food because it was a long journey.
Check: All sentences are correctly punctuated.

Pupil book answers

Writing with joining words

Remember

You can use **joining words** to help improve your writing. Joining words can join two ideas together to make one longer **sentence**.

My dog likes to run around outside but he does not like having a bath. I take him for a walk every day because he needs lots of exercise.

Try it

1 Complete each sentence with a suitable **joining word**. Use a different one each time.

Dad got in the car _____and_____ he drove to work.

She tried on the shoe _____but_____ it did not fit.

Craig was crying _____because_____ he was lost.

Rebecca hopes _____that_____ she will win the game.

Cross the road _____when_____ you see the cars stop.

> Accept alternative conjunctions to those shown if they make grammatical sense, but check that a different word has been used each time.

2 Write each pair of sentences as <u>one</u> sentence, using a **joining word**.

Sonia went to the dentist. She had a bad tooth.

Sonia went to the dentist because she had a bad tooth.

I know it is home time. I hear the bell ring.

I know it is home time when I hear the bell ring.

> Accept alternative conjunctions if they make grammatical sense.
>
> Check that the sentences are correctly punctuated.

Sentence practice

Write <u>two</u> sentences about reading books. Use a **joining word** in each one.

I like reading books when I go to bed. I like funny books best because

they cheer me up.

41

> These are just examples. Any conjunction can be used.
> Check that the sentences are correctly punctuated.

Revision 3 answers

Focus: commas in lists

Check that there is no comma after 'France'. Other punctuation [capital letters and full stop] should have been copied correctly.

These pages revise concepts introduced earlier in this book. The focus of each activity is given to help identify areas that may need further reinforcement.

Revision 3

1 Write this sentence with the correct **punctuation**.

My brother has been to Spain France and Italy.

My brother has been to Spain, France and Italy.

Focus: forming adjectives using suffixes –er, –est

These are just examples of suitable adjectives. Other words also fit the sentences. The first and third answers must be comparatives [ending –er]; the second and fourth must be superlatives [ending –est].

Accept adjectives that make sense even if they do not fit the regular pattern for these suffixes [e.g. better, best].

2 Add a suitable **adjective** to complete each sentence.

An elephant is ___bigger___ than a mouse.

The sun is the ___brightest___ thing in the sky.

An orange is ___sweeter___ than a lime.

Ava is the ___cleverest___ girl in our class.

3 Use a **joining word** to complete each sentence. Use 'or', 'but', 'that' or 'if'.

She ran so fast ___that___ he could not catch her.

The glass will break ___if___ you drop it.

Eat your lunch ___or___ you will be hungry.

I want to stay up ___but___ it is late.

Focus: subordinating conjunctions 'when', 'if', 'that', 'because'

If necessary, remind pupils to choose the word that links the two parts of the sentence so that it makes sense.

4 Use all of these nouns to make <u>five</u> **compound nouns**. Write each new compound noun.

table	paper	tablecloth
news	barrow	newspaper
gold	rope	goldfish
wheel	cloth	wheelbarrow
tight	fish	tightrope

42

Focus: forming compound nouns

The answers must be written as one word with no space between the two smaller words.

Check that all words are compound nouns, rather than two-noun phrases [e.g. gold paper].

5 Add a **suffix** to make each word into an **adjective**.

spite ful   end less   play ful

Now use the **adjectives** to complete these **noun phrases**.

the _____ playful _____ little kitten

the mean and _____ spiteful _____ man

the _____ endless _____ list of jobs

6 Complete each sentence using the **–ing** form of a **verb**.

I was wiping the table and Leon _____ was washing _____ the dishes.

It is raining and I _____ am getting _____ wet.

It happened when Dad _____ was parking _____ the car.

We saw a fox when we _____ were walking _____ the dog.

7 Rewrite each sentence using an **adjective** to describe the **noun**.

I saw a spider. I saw a huge spider.

What a room! What a messy room!

There was a storm. There was a noisy storm.

She had three brothers. She had three silly brothers.

8 Complete these sentences.

I wanted an ice cream but there were none left.

I need my gloves because it is cold today.

Sita ran home when it was time for dinner.

Dad will take us to the fairground if we are lucky.

43

Focus: forming adjectives using suffixes –ful, –less

The adjectives must be spelt correctly – both root word and suffix.

Focus: using progressive forms of verbs in past and present tense

This activity also checks that the children understand the need for tense consistency.

Other verbs can be used but they must be in the progressive form and use the correct tense.

Focus: using adjectives in noun phrases for description

Any suitable adjective is acceptable, although you may wish to discuss good descriptive choices. Accept also sentences that use two adjectives.

Focus: co-ordinating and subordinating conjunctions 'but', 'because', 'when'

These are examples of suitable sentence endings. The sentences must make sense, be grammatically correct and end with full stops.

Writing task 3: Analysis sheet

Tick the circles to show amount
of evidence found in writing:
1 No evidence
2 Some evidence
3 Clear evidence

Pupil name: _____

Date: _____

Assessing punctuation

The writing sample demonstrates:	Evidence		
capital letters used at the beginning of sentences.	①	②	③
sentence boundaries recognised and demarcated with full stops.	①	②	③
question marks and exclamation marks used appropriately when required.	①	②	③
capital letters used for 'I' and proper nouns [e.g. names of characters].	①	②	③
commas used to separate items in a list [e.g. It was yellow, red and purple.].	①	②	③
apostrophes used in contracted forms or for possession [e.g. Mum's car].	①	②	③

Assessing grammar and sentence structure

The writing sample demonstrates:	Evidence		
grammatically correct sentences.	①	②	③
different sentence types [e.g. statements; exclamations – 'What a shock!'].	①	②	③
co-ordinating conjunctions [and, but, or] to join clauses.	①	②	③
subordinating conjunctions [because, when, if, that] to add more detail [e.g. Mum jumped when she saw me.].	①	②	③
correct and consistent use of past tense, including progressive forms.	①	②	③
appropriate use of adjectives and adverbs [e.g. I quickly took a sip from the little bottle.].	①	②	③
expanded noun phrases to describe and specify [e.g. the smallest flower in the garden; the little blue bottle with the yellow label].	①	②	③

Key target: _____

From: **Grammar 2 Teacher's Guide** © *Schofield & Sims Ltd, 2017. This page may be photocopied after purchase.*

Writing task 3: Pupil checklist

Name: _____   Date: _____

Reread what you have written to check that it makes sense. Tick the circle if you have correctly used the punctuation or grammar feature in your writing.

Punctuation

- ( ) I have used capital letters at the beginning of sentences.
- ( ) I have used full stops at the end of sentences.
- ( ) I have used a question mark or exclamation mark if it is needed.
- ( ) I have used capital letters for 'I' and any names.
- ( ) I have used commas to separate items in a list.
- ( ) I have used apostrophes when they are needed.

Grammar and sentences

- ( ) I have written in sentences and they make sense.
- ( ) I have used different types of sentence (statements, questions, exclamations, commands).
- ( ) I have used 'and', 'but', 'or' to make some longer sentences.
- ( ) I have used 'because', 'when', 'that', 'if' to add more information to a sentence.
- ( ) I have used the past tense all through my story.
- ( ) I have used some adjectives and some adverbs.
- ( ) I have used some longer noun phrases (for example, the little blue bottle with the yellow label).

Teacher feedback

My key target: _____

_____

From: **Grammar 2 Teacher's Guide** © Schofield & Sims Ltd, 2017. This page may be photocopied after purchase.

Final test

Name: _____

1 Add the missing **punctuation mark** to each sentence.

I have an idea _____   I went for a run _____

What is it _____   Where did you go _____

1 mark

2 Tick the correct word to complete the sentence below.

I wanted an apple _____ the bowl was empty.

and ☐   or ☐   but ☐   if ☐

1 mark

3 Tick the sentence with the correct **punctuation**.

I want Amit Ella Marie, and Lucas in my group. ☐

I want Amit, Ella, Marie and Lucas in my group. ☐

I want Amit, Ella, Marie, and Lucas, in my group. ☐

1 mark

4 What type of word is underlined in the sentence below?

The cat chased the mouse into the <u>long</u> grass.

verb ☐   adjective ☐   noun ☐   adverb ☐

1 mark

5 Circle the <u>three</u> **nouns** in the sentence below.

The hairy caterpillar nibbled a hole in the biggest leaf.

1 mark

From: **Grammar 2 Teacher's Guide** © *Schofield & Sims Ltd, 2017. This page may be photocopied after purchase.*

6 Draw lines to match the **sentence** to the correct sentence type.

Put the book on the shelf. ●

I have a book to read. ●

Read me a story. ●

The teacher reads a story. ●

| statement |
| command |

1 mark

7 Tick <u>two</u> boxes to show the **verbs** in the sentence below.

We walked a long way and I was tired by the end.

1 mark

8 Why do the underlined words end with –s?

We watched the <u>horses</u> jumping wooden <u>fences</u>.

_____

1 mark

9 Complete the sentence below using an **adverb**.

The boy walked _____ home.

1 mark

10 The **verbs** in this sentence are in the **present tense**. Write these verbs in the **past tense**.

Granddad bakes a cake and we eat it for tea.

_____   _____

1 mark

From: **Grammar 2 Teacher's Guide** © Schofield & Sims Ltd, 2017. This page may be photocopied after purchase.

11 Tick the correct word to complete the sentence below.

Molly was feeling ill _____ she got up this morning.

because ☐   if ☐   that ☐   when ☐

1 mark

12 Tick <u>one</u> box to show where a **full stop** should go.

I played with Joe and Harry Lucy joined in.

☐   ☐   ☐   ☐

1 mark

13 Underline the words that should start with a **capital letter** in the sentence below.

My brother jake went to richmond park on saturday.

1 mark

14 Tick the correct box to show the **tense** of each sentence.

	Past tense	Present tense
I am having a rest.		
Jess was playing on the swings.		
Daniel is racing Ben.		

1 mark

15 Add a **suffix** to make each word a **noun**.

a buzz_____   a punish_____   a sick_____

1 mark

From: **Grammar 2 Teacher's Guide** © Schofield & Sims Ltd, 2017. This page may be photocopied after purchase.

16 Tick the sentence that is correct.

Omar plays on the beach and swam in the sea. ☐

Omar plays on the beach and swim in the sea. ☐

Omar played on the beach and swam in the sea. ☐

☐

1 mark

17 Write the words 'I will' as one word, using an **apostrophe**.

_____ see you soon.

☐

1 mark

18 Rewrite the sentence correctly, using an **apostrophe**.

Have you seen Dad toothbrush?

_____

☐

1 mark

19 Write a sentence with this **noun phrase** in it.

the old house

_____

☐

1 mark

20 Tick the correct word to complete the sentence below.

It is _____ in here than outside.

warm ☐   warmly ☐   warmer ☐   warmest ☐

☐

1 mark

End of test

From: **Grammar 2 Teacher's Guide** © *Schofield & Sims Ltd, 2017. This page may be photocopied after purchase.*

Final test: Mark scheme

Q	Focus	Answer
1	full stops, question marks, exclamation marks	**Award 1 mark** for all <u>four</u> punctuation marks correctly added. I have an idea. What is it? I went for a run. Where did you go?
2	co-ordinating conjunctions	**Award 1 mark** for the correct box ticked. but ✓
3	commas to separate items in a list	**Award 1 mark** for the correct box ticked. I want Amit, Ella, Marie and Lucas in my group. ✓
4	identifying adjectives	**Award 1 mark** for the correct box ticked. adjective ✓
5	identifying nouns	**Award 1 mark** for all <u>three</u> correctly identified. The hairy <u>caterpillar</u> nibbled a <u>hole</u> in the biggest <u>leaf</u>.
6	sentence type: commands and statements	**Award 1 mark** for all <u>four</u> matched correctly. Put the book on the shelf. ●　　　● statement I have a book to read. ● Read me a story. ●　　　● command The teacher reads a story. ●
7	identifying verbs	**Award 1 mark** for <u>both</u> boxes ticked. We walked a long way and I was tired by the end. 　　　　↑　　　　　　↑ 　　　　✓　　　　　　✓
8	plural noun suffixes –s, –es	**Award 1 mark** for answers explaining that the words end with –s because they are plurals, e.g. because there was more than one horse and fence because you put an 's' on the end if there is more than one
9	forming and using adverbs ending with –ly	**Award 1 mark** for any appropriate adverb, e.g. slowly; quickly; sadly; happily Adverbs ending with –ly must be spelt correctly.
10	forming simple past tense verbs	**Award 1 mark** for <u>both</u> words. baked　　ate The past tense verbs must be spelt correctly.
11	subordinating conjunctions	**Award 1 mark** for the correct box ticked. when ✓
12	demarcating sentences with full stops	**Award 1 mark** for the correct box ticked. I played with Joe and Harry Lucy joined in. 　　　　　　　　↑ 　　　　　　　　✓

13	capital letters for names, days of the week	**Award 1 mark** for all <u>four</u> words correctly identified. My brother <u>jake</u> went to <u>richmond park</u> on <u>saturday</u>.
14	present and past progressive forms	**Award 1 mark** for all <u>three</u> correct.

	Past tense	Present tense
I am having a rest.		✓
Jess was playing on the swings.	✓	
Daniel is racing Ben.		✓

15	forming nouns with suffixes –ness, –ment, –er	**Award 1 mark** for all <u>three</u> correct suffixes added. a buzzer, a punishment, a sickness
16	consistent use of tense	**Award 1 mark** for the correct box ticked. Omar played on the beach and swam in the sea. ✓
17	apostrophes to mark contracted forms	**Award 1 mark** for: I'll Correct spelling and correct placement of the apostrophe are required. 'I' must be written as a capital letter.
18	apostrophes to mark possession	**Award 1 mark** for the sentence rewritten with the apostrophe in the correct position. Have you seen Dad's toothbrush?
19	combining words to make sentences	**Award 1 mark** for an appropriate sentence that also starts with a capital letter and ends with a full stop, e.g. The old house looked spooky. The old house had a red door. I found the old house on a hill. We went inside the old house.
20	adjectives using suffixes –er and –est	**Award 1 mark** for the correct box ticked. warmer ✓

Final test: Analysis sheet

Tick the box for each correct answer.

Q	Focus	Pupil names									
1	full stops, question marks, exclamation marks										
2	co-ordinating conjunctions										
3	commas to separate items in a list										
4	identifying adjectives										
5	sentence type: commands and statements										
6	identifying nouns										
7	identifying verbs										
8	plural noun suffixes –s, –es										
9	forming and using adverbs ending with –ly										
10	forming simple past tense verbs										
11	subordinating conjunctions										
12	demarcating sentences with full stops										
13	capital letters for names, days of the week										
14	present and past progressive forms										
15	forming nouns with suffixes –ness, –ment, –er										
16	consistent use of tense										
17	apostrophes to mark contracted forms										
18	apostrophes to mark possession										
19	combining words to make sentences										
20	adjectives using suffixes –er and –est										
	Total correct answers per pupil										

*From: **Grammar 2 Teacher's Guide** © Schofield & Sims Ltd, 2017. This page may be photocopied after purchase.*

Target tracking sheet

Group: _____

Target: _____

Date: _____   Date for review: _____

Tick the circles to show depth of understanding:
1 Just beginning
2 Progressing
3 Learning is embedded

Pupil name	Evidence from independent writing	Progress in independent writing		
		①	②	③
		①	②	③
		①	②	③
		①	②	③
		①	②	③
		①	②	③
		①	②	③
		①	②	③
		①	②	③
		①	②	③

From: **Grammar 2 Teacher's Guide** © *Schofield & Sims Ltd, 2017. This page may be photocopied after purchase.*

Learning pathways sheet

Pupil name: _____

Date last updated: _____

Tick the circles to show depth of understanding:

1 Just beginning
2 Progressing
3 Learning is embedded

(3) ✓

Punctuation pathway

Use capital letters at the start of sentences.

(1) (2) (3)

Recognise and demarcate sentence boundaries with full stops.

(1) (2) (3)

Use question marks and exclamation marks to demarcate different sentence types.

(1) (2) (3)

Use capital letters for 'I' and all proper nouns [names of people, places, days of the week].

(1) (2) (3)

Use commas to separate items in a list.

(1) (2) (3)

Use apostrophes in shortened (contracted) forms.

(1) (2) (3)

Use apostrophes for (singular) possession.

(1) (2) (3)

Grammar and sentence pathway

Form sentences that are complete and correct.

(1) (2) (3)

Use the words 'and', 'but', 'or' to join clauses within sentences.

(1) (2) (3)

Use different sentence types as appropriate: command, question, exclamation, statement.

(1) (2) (3)

Use past or present tense consistently, including use of progressive forms.

(1) (2) (3)

Use words such as 'because' 'if' 'when' 'that' to add more to a sentence.

(1) (2) (3)

Use adjectives in expanded noun phrases to describe or specify.

(1) (2) (3)

Use adverbs where appropriate to describe how actions are performed.

(1) (2) (3)

From: **Grammar 2 Teacher's Guide** © *Schofield & Sims Ltd, 2017. This page may be photocopied after purchase.*

Glossary

Adjective

An **adjective** is a word used to modify or specify a noun [e.g. an <u>angry</u> man; the <u>red</u> car]. Lesson 12
- Some adjectives are formed by adding a suffix to a word [e.g. care<u>ful</u>; care<u>less</u>]. Lesson 13
- The suffixes –er and –est are used to form **comparative** adjectives [e.g. smaller] and **superlative** adjectives [e.g. smallest]. These adjectives are used when comparing nouns. Lesson 14

Adverb

An **adverb** is a word that modifies a verb or action, for example, saying *how* the action is performed [e.g. He sat <u>quietly</u>. The ship sailed <u>smoothly</u>.]. Lesson 21

Many adverbs are formed by adding the suffix –ly to an adjective [e.g. kind<u>ly</u>]. However, not all adverbs end with –ly [e.g. She stood <u>still</u>. She ran <u>fast</u>.]. Lesson 22

Apostrophe

An **apostrophe [']** is a punctuation mark used:
- to show missing letters in **shortened forms** [contractions] [e.g. can't]. Lesson 23
- to show **possession** [e.g. Sam's hat]. Lesson 24

Comma

A **comma [,]** is a punctuation mark used within sentences [e.g. to separate items in a list]. Lesson 18

Conjunction

A **conjunction** is a word that joins two words or clauses together [e.g. and, but; because, when]. In Grammar 1 and Grammar 2 the phrase 'joining word' is used in place of 'conjunction'.

There are two types of conjunction, although pupils do not need to know this terminology in Key Stage 1:
- **co-ordinating conjunctions** [and, but, or]. Lessons 3 and 4;
- **subordinating conjunctions** [e.g. because; when; if]. Lessons 15, 16 and 30

Noun

Nouns are words that name things, places, people [e.g. car; park; man]. These are **common nouns**. Lesson 11
- **Proper nouns** are the names of specific people, places or things [e.g. Joe; Banbury Park; July]. Proper nouns start with a capital letter. Lesson 26
- A **compound noun** is a noun made up of two root words joined together [e.g. footpath]. Lesson 17
- A **noun phrase** is a group of words that expand on a noun [e.g. car → the fast police car]. The other words added to the noun 'car' tell us more about it. Lessons 11, 12 and 29

Prefixes and suffixes

A **prefix** is added to the start of a word to make it into another word [e.g. <u>un</u>do].
A **suffix** is added to the end of a word to change how we use the word [e.g. forming adjectives – peace<u>ful</u>; harm<u>less</u> or nouns – amaze<u>ment</u>]. Lessons 13 and 25

Sentence

A **sentence** is a group of words connected together that makes sense/says something. A sentence starts with a capital letter and ends with a full stop [or '?' or '!']. Lesson 1

There are different forms of sentence with different functions and different grammatical patterns:

- **Statements** give information. They usually start with subject–verb [e.g. <u>Joe ran</u> away. <u>It is</u> cold today.]. Lesson 7
- **Questions** ask for information or need a response. They begin with a question word or a subject–verb reversal and end with question mark [e.g. <u>What</u> is the weather like today? <u>Is it</u> cold today?]. Lesson 8
- **Exclamations** express strong emotion and end with an exclamation mark. A strict definition of an exclamation refers to sentences starting with 'What' or 'How' [e.g. What a surprise! How amazing!]. However, interjections are also exclamatory [e.g. Oh dear!]. Lesson 9
- **Commands** direct someone to do something. The main clause often starts with a verb [e.g. Come here.]. Lesson 10

We sometimes add exclamation marks to statements or commands to make exclamatory statements or exclamatory commands [e.g. It was great! Help!]. However, this does not change the form of the sentence.

Sentence punctuation

Sentence punctuation refers to the use of capital letters, full stops, question marks and exclamation marks to show the boundaries between sentences.

- **Capital letters** are used to mark the beginning of a sentence. They are also used at the start of names and for the word 'I'. Lessons 1 and 2
- A **full stop** is used to mark the end of a sentence. Lessons 1 and 2
- A **question mark [?]** is used in place of a full stop if a sentence is a question. Lesson 2
- An **exclamation mark [!]** is used if the sentence is an exclamation or to show strong feeling. Lesson 2

Singular and plural

Many nouns have singular and plural forms. **Singular** means there is just one of something; **plural** means there is more than one of something. Plural forms are usually formed by adding –s or –es to the noun [e.g. cat<u>s</u>; dog<u>s</u>; fox<u>es</u>]. Lesson 27

Verb

A verb is a 'doing' or 'being' word [e.g. He <u>ran</u>. He <u>is</u> sad.]. Verbs are important because they tell us about the actions in a sentence.

- Verbs in a sentence usually have a **tense**. The tense of a verb tells us *when* the action happened – in the **past** or the **present**. Many simple **past tense verbs** are formed by adding –ed [e.g. jumped; stopped]. Other verbs have irregular **past tense** forms [e.g. have/had; see/saw]. Lessons 5, 6 and 28
- **Progressive forms** (also called 'continuous') can be used in the present and past tense to describe events in progress, or events that were in progress, for some time. They use the –ing form of the verb with the helper verb is/are/am or was/were [e.g. he <u>is</u> sing<u>ing</u>; she <u>was</u> walk<u>ing</u>]. Lessons 19 and 20